EKKLESIA
GROUP GUIDE

Books by Ed Silvoso

That None Should Perish
Prayer Evangelism
Women: God's Secret Weapon
Anointed for Business
Transformation
Ekklesia

EKKLESIA

— GROUP GUIDE —

REDISCOVERING
GOD'S INSTRUMENT
FOR GLOBAL
TRANSFORMATION

ED
SILVOSO

Chosen
a division of Baker Publishing Group
Minneapolis, Minnesota

Published by Chosen Books
11400 Hampshire Avenue South
Bloomington, Minnesota 55438
www.chosenbooks.com

Chosen Books is a division of
Baker Publishing Group, Grand Rapids, Michigan

Printed in the United States of America

Library of Congress Control Number: 2017934419

ISBN 9780800798475

Cover design by Dan Pitts

17 18 19 20 21 22 23   7 6 5 4 3 2 1

Contents

Ekklesia Group Roster

Name	Phone	Email
1.		
2.		
3.		
4.		
5.		
6.		
7.		
8.		
9.		
10.		
11.		
12.		

Introduction

This *Ekklesia Group Guide* and its accompanying video segments on DVD are designed for use in connection with my book *Ekklesia: Rediscovering God's Instrument for Global Transformation*. The intention in providing this curriculum is to enable the reader to go deeper in an understanding of the spiritual principles in the book, and especially to go deeper in the application of these principles to living a transformation lifestyle. The overarching theme of this whole study is how to take the power and the presence of God to your sphere of influence and for God to perform extraordinary miracles through you.

I was blessed to partner with Dr. Greg Pagh, senior pastor of Christ Church in Otsego, Minnesota, to produce this material. He is a minister who loves the people who sit under his teaching as much as he loves the people outside the four walls of the church who don't know the Lord. He is also a respected Bible teacher.

The addition of Dave Thompson greatly enhanced our partnership. Dave has worked with me, pioneering transformation, for over thirty years. He was in Argentina when we built the prayer chapel that came to define the genesis of our movement. He was also in Resistencia, the city where we put to the test the principles we learned, and from where the principles went out to the world. Dave understands pastors and marketplace ministers in a way few people do, and he brings the informed perspective of someone whom I consider "the keeper and the nurturer of the vision" of our ministry. His contributions have proven invaluable.

A team of pastors and marketplace ministers who are top-notch practitioners of transformation also assisted us by contributing their very helpful observations: Caroline Oda, Poncho Murguía, Brian Burton, Barbara Chan and Wong Po Ling. I know that the result of our team effort, in which everyone generously contributed what the Lord has entrusted to them, will bless you.

It is our desire that the *Ekklesia* book and its accompanying curriculum, of which this group guide is an important component, will be an encouragement to pastors who wish to see the people under their care experience Bible-based, Spirit-led transformation at a personal level, at home and in their spheres of influence. We especially desire that what we are presenting will encourage those who spend the bulk of their time in the marketplace, so that they will realize they are also ministers—a realization that will result in a stronger partnership with their pastors and fellow believers.

It is our hope that all this will lead to the establishment of myriads of Ekklesia groups in the marketplace, as a growing number of believers learn to take the power and presence of God with them into the workplace and everywhere they go for the will of God to be done on earth, as it is already done in heaven.

Group leaders for this study will need all three parts of the curriculum—the *Ekklesia* book, the group guide and the companion DVDs. To that effect, we have made available an *Ekklesia* curriculum kit that contains all three. Participants will need at least the book and the group guide to use as a workbook, although individuals could also benefit from having the DVDs. The DVDs are designed to provide *Ekklesia* study groups with a brief and inspiring overview of the material and key points for each session. Whether you are a group leader, a participant or are working through *Ekklesia* yourself, you can acquire the book, the group guide and the DVDs individually or in the kit. Leaders can also supplement this curriculum by accessing the additional training materials we offer on our website at https://transformourworld.org/transformationondemand/store/.

We are aware that certain logistical matters must be taken care of when launching a study group. We chose to leave the internal organizational aspects of each group to the leaders, since different groups will meet in a variety of venues: homes, businesses, schools, government buildings, parks and elsewhere. Some groups may meet during business hours, and others after work. Some groups may need child care available, and others will not. Some groups may want to include worship in their routine, and others will choose to go straight into the study of the material. Each group should find the best way to work through these logistical details.

As I stated in the preface of *Ekklesia*, writing this book has led me into the most stimulating Bible journey I have ever been on. It is my prayer, along with that of Dr. Pagh, Dave Thompson and the team who made this group guide possible, that you will have a similar, and even richer, experience.

May the Lord richly bless you!

Ed Silvoso, author, *Ekklesia*

Series Overview

As you work through this *Ekklesia Group Guide* yourself or lead a study group through these materials, here are some helpful things you should know. We based each of the twelve sessions in this guide on one or two chapters in my *Ekklesia* book. This guide's table of contents identifies which chapters each session covers. I strongly encourage every group participant to read the relevant chapters at least once before participating in the related study session.

Ekklesia study groups, or "eGroups," as we will call them, generally will consist of up to twelve individuals meeting in a setting of their choice, whether in a church, a home, someone's workplace, a school, a coffee shop or wherever works best for their group. (I will address group size further in "A Word to Leaders" just ahead.) This guide will take the group on a "deep dive" into the biblical principles of the *Ekklesia* teaching, and then help each participant learn to apply these principles in his or her personal spheres of influence in a city, region and nation.

Depending on the size of your eGroup and the amount of time you give to discussion and prayer, each session will require a minimum of one hour of group time. That is the ideal time frame in which to cover each session, but if your group meeting is shorter, you can still cover the material in an abbreviated format. For example, if your eGroup is meeting in a market-place setting over lunch, I recommend that the group leader highlight some key points in the **Transformed Thinking** section of the session, cover the **Session Summary**, and then focus on three general questions:

- What did the book chapter(s) say?
- What did this session's transformation principles say to me?
- What action should I/we take on a personal/group level?

Even in an abbreviated format, it is important that every eGroup take time for prayer and ministry. It is also important that both personally and as a group, participants embrace the **Life Applications** in the **Transformed Living** section so that they will be able to apply the principles in each lesson.

Every session in this guide includes the following main sections:

Introduction: To learn what the session is about and what you will walk away with.

Sharing Life: To connect with your eGroup as you watch the session's introduction video together, pray at the start of your meeting, and review your progress in the weekly **Life Applications**.

Transformed Thinking: To review and discuss key biblical principles from the book, including summary material, Scripture references, inspiring quotes and prototypes, and testimonies from around the world.

Session Summary: To review and reflect on the session's highlights.

Transformed Living: To apply the *Ekklesia* teaching through **Life Applications**, both personally and as an eGroup.

Ekklesia Prayer and Ministry: To engage in group prayer and personal ministry.

Reading Assignment: To become informed about what chapter(s) to read prior to the next session.

Daily Devotions: To dig deeper during the coming week through the use of additional Bible references related to the session.

Again, it is recommended that each *Ekklesia* study group participant have his or her own copy of this group guide. In it, we have provided space for noting responses to discussion questions and writing down personal reflections, ideas for application, prayer requests and more. This guide will serve as a valuable tool for you as you discover what it means to become part of Jesus' Ekklesia and establish a transformation lifestyle. Enjoy the journey!

A Word to Leaders

Thank you for accepting the call to serve as an eGroup leader. You will fulfill an important role in guiding your group through this study so that participants will receive not only excellent teaching but also an impartation from the Holy Spirit that will change their lives forever! As participants learn to take the power and presence of God into their spheres of influence in the marketplace, cities and nations will begin to be discipled in Jesus' name.

As noted in the "Series Overview," eGroups may meet in a variety of venues. One place might be the local church, perhaps as part of a sermon/teaching series based on the book. The preferred location, however, is in the marketplace. Even as you move through this twelve-session study, encourage the participants in your group to consider future opportunities to establish eGroups in business, education and government settings. Additional resources to help with this are available on the Transform Our World website and in our online store.

For the purposes of building relationships, sharing in lively group discussion and taking meaningful action steps together, the ideal size for an eGroup is seven to twelve people. If your group is smaller, however, even from three to five members, embrace the opportunity to grow from there.

If your group exceeds twelve, the dynamics will change and it will become a class rather than a small group. You could present this material in a class format, but you will need to make some adjustments to allow for that. For example, you could use this group guide in a church setting for a one-hour adult class, but that will challenge you with a shorter time frame and a higher number of participants, which can limit your teaching time and group discussion. To offset these challenges, you can ask participants to work through the study sessions during the week. Then with the time you have available in your eGroup, you can watch the DVD together, highlight key teaching points, engage the group in as much discussion as possible, and encourage personal/group application of the transformation principles. Marketplace groups facing a similar time crunch can also get creative with this material in the same ways. As the leader, use this group guide in whatever way you find is most effective and helpful to engage people in the *Ekklesia* teaching and application in your local setting.

You will discover that there is a minimal amount of "direction giving" in this group guide, in order to provide you with the greatest flexibility for your eGroup. As you prepare to lead your group, please work through each session in advance so that you are familiar with its contents and flow. Also personally think about the discussion questions in advance. Discussion questions are captioned either **Share** or **Deeper.** Depending on time availability, reflect on the **Share** questions as a group and encourage participants to utilize the **Deeper** questions for further reflection on their own.

Don't dwell on any question too long in your group. Keep the discussion moving. Not everyone needs to answer every question. Once there have been some good responses, move on to the next section. Try to draw out those participants who may be quieter. Avoid the temptation to talk too much as the leader or comment on every person's response. Be flexible and open to "Holy Spirit moments" and "God surprises" that may even lead you to pause for prayer or ministry.

The **Read** sections provide you with opportunities to engage the members of your eGroup. You can ask for volunteers to read out loud or take turns reading. In some places, you are encouraged to read out loud together as a group. Don't put anyone on the spot, but try to involve as many in your group as possible.

To be effective, *each session must be bathed in prayer and the power of the Holy Spirit.* I encourage you to pray for your eGroup members every day, as they will be asked to do for one another. Ask the Lord to give you wisdom in facilitating each session to gain maximum participation, engagement and impact for the Kingdom of God. As you share together, the Holy Spirit will open up opportunities for ministry to take place within your group. Remind your group of the importance of confidentiality when personal matters are shared. Help create a fun and accepting atmosphere of growing together in Christ.

The **Ekklesia Prayer and Ministry** time at the end of each session is one place in particular where, as the leader, your sensitivity to the Holy Spirit is crucial. He is your leader as you lead the group. Participants will be sharing prayer requests and testimonies. Go beyond simple closing prayers and minister to the members of the group for whatever needs they have identified. For example, you may gather around a group member in need of healing or encouragement, lay hands on him or her and offer prayers of faith. Teach the group by your example as a leader so they can grow in their confidence about ministering in other settings. Encourage them to continue their ministry throughout the week.

The **Life Applications**, both personal and group, are a key component of this study. Application is where the rubber meets the road! Throughout this curriculum and in my series of transformation books, I emphasize the principles of prayer evangelism as a *lifestyle*, not a program. The applications will help participants adopt these principles as their lifestyle.

I will give more detail about each application in the sessions that follow, but in general, the **Personal Life Applications** allow individual participants to apply the *Ekklesia* teaching in very practical ways within their own spheres of influence: family, neighbors, workplace, school, etc. These personal applications are designed to help eGroup members reflect on their personal relationship with God, develop the skills necessary to reach out to others, and grow in confidence as members of Jesus' Ekklesia.

The **Group Life Applications** take the application of transformation paradigms and principles deeper and wider, to touch the city or region your eGroup meets in through group projects. One strategic focus will be to identify an unreconciled "social gap" in your area and respond as a group with tangible acts of kindness, matching words with deeds and asking God for miracles to heal that gap.

As the group leader, part of your task will be to oversee these action steps and provide loving accountability, encouragement and support to eGroup members. At the end of the twelve sessions, the goal is that every person will have a greater vision for reaching his or her city for Christ. Participants will finish the study knowing that God wants to use them in this process as a member of Jesus' Ekklesia, and they will have "tracks to run on" to continue this transformation journey and see it expand.

Thank you again for your willingness to serve as an eGroup leader. Depending on your setting and the focus of your particular study group, you may have a pastor or marketplace leader providing you with oversight, support and encouragement in this process. If so, make use of these leaders to help you grow in your own leadership. May God bless you abundantly!

Session	Personal Life Application	Group Life Application
1.	Prayer Evangelism—Step 1—*Bless* Bless and speak peace to those people in your spheres of influence.	Pray daily for those in your eGroup by name and "bless and speak peace over them." Plan an eGroup meal and invite others to join you.
2.	Prayer Evangelism—Step 2—*Fellowship* Continue step 1. Fellowship with a new friend over a cup of coffee or a meal to build relationships.	Follow up with your personal guests who attended the eGroup meal by contacting them via an encouraging text, email or phone call to continue to build relationships.
3.	Prayer Evangelism—Step 3—*Minister* Continue steps 1 and 2. Identify the felt needs in the life of your new friend(s). Respond with prayers of faith and action.	As a group, see how many times this week you have the opportunity to make the declaration "the Kingdom of God has come near to you!" in your spheres of influence.
4.	Prayer Evangelism—Step 4—*Proclaim* Continue steps 1 through 3. As the Holy Spirit opens doors, share your transformation testimony with your new friends.	Identify a "social gap" in your city/region that your eGroup will respond to. Pray and gather information. Identify the felt needs of those affected by the social gap and consider how your group can match words with deeds.
5.	Continue to develop a lifestyle of prayer evangelism. Memorize: John 3:16–17 Matthew 22:37–39 Matthew 28:18–20	Continue practicing prayer evangelism in relationship to your group's targeted social gap. Minister to the felt needs you have identified, expecting miracles, and proclaim the Kingdom of God.
6.	*Adopt Your Street* in prayer at http://adopt.transformour world.org/en/adopt. Use this strategy to continue to implement the principles of prayer evangelism with a strategic focus.	Proclaim the Good News, going to a "high place" in your city or region and declaring a spirit of adoption over it.
7.	Write a personal note of encouragement to a marketplace minister in your city or region. Do a deed that puts the *real* Jesus on display.	Watch the video *Transformation in Brantford, Canada* at www.transformourworld.org. (Click on "Transformation on Demand" to sign up for viewing.)
8.	If you have not yet been baptized in water, please consider doing so by talking to your pastor or eGroup leader. Invite prayer for a fresh baptism in the Holy Spirit.	Continue to *bapto* and *baptizo* your city, putting deeds to your words. Go from "dipping" to "dripping"!
9.	Since Jesus honored women as equals before God and partners in ministry, find a special way to celebrate several women who have been significant in your life, utilizing the principles of prayer evangelism.	Do a food and clothing drive (or similar project) within your local Ekklesia to bless your city. Consider how you can respond to all four aspects of systemic poverty in some way.
10.	Claim your spiritual authority and important role as a marketplace minister and ask God to use you to change the spiritual climate in your workplace.	Seek God in prayer for miracles in the marketplace that will provide divine solutions and lead others to Christ.
11.	Reflect on the paradigms and principles of transformation as you sit near a local river. Do a soul-searching assessment of your current relationship with God.	Plan an eGroup celebration as your *Ekklesia* twelve-week study nears an end.
12.	Consider "the way forward" for you as a member of Jesus' Ekklesia.	Consider "next steps" and what kind of resources and support are available to grow and multiply your eGroup.

SESSION 1

What this lesson is about:

Jesus did not say "I will build My Temple" or "I will build My synagogue"—the two most prominent Jewish religious institutions of His time. Instead, He chose a secular entity first developed by the Greeks when He said, "I will build My Ekklesia." Why? The answer is fascinating, challenging and empowering!

What you will walk away with:

First, you will be reminded that the Church is always people, not buildings, and you will discover exciting dimensions of the Church to make it effective and victorious in the public arena and not just inside four walls. You will understand that in the same manner that the Roman Empire made its presence and power felt even in the far reaches of its territory, Jesus designed His Ekklesia to make His presence and power known all over the world, but with a revolutionary caveat that gave it the upper hand over evil: *It would have the authority to legislate in both the visible and invisible realms* so that the Gates of Hades could not prevail against it in either realm.

Sharing Life

Watch: Play the video introduction for Session 1. This session is based on the introduction and chapter 1 in my book *Ekklesia*, "Church: A Radical Proposition."

Share: A very important aspect of being the Ekklesia is the development of meaningful relationships that reflect the love of Jesus. To get to know your eGroup, take turns sharing briefly:

- Your name
- Your family information
- Where you live
- What you do for work or how you spend your time
- What local church you attend
- One reason why you are excited to be part of this study

Read: The "textbook" for this group guide is my book *Ekklesia: Rediscovering God's Instrument for Global Transformation*. In the introduction of the book, I make the statement that "the Church is the only institution on earth that has a branch in every city and a representative in every neighborhood."

Share: Give some examples of expressions of the Church that can be found in the neighborhood or city where you live (congregations, ministry organizations, hospitals, counseling centers, food shelves, homeless shelters and the like).

_____

_____

Read: As you join this Ekklesia group, remember that you are not alone. You will have the support of others, especially your leaders and your fellow group participants. Most importantly, you will have the support of your heavenly Father, who loves you and wants the very best for your life.

As I also say in the book's introduction, the biblical principles you will read about, along with the validating testimonies and case studies in the book, will inspire you and will lead you to a victorious *lifestyle* in your own journey, in your family and in your sphere of influence. Join your hearts together and share in the following group prayer of dedication.

Pray Together: Dear God, thank You for this beautiful world You have created and for everything in it. We know that You love it so much. Would You please show us how to love it, too? During these next twelve weeks, we want to hear Your voice and learn from Your Word. We ask that You anoint us with Your Holy Spirit so that under His leading and promptings, we will discover the deeper meaning and purpose of Jesus' Ekklesia. Help us move beyond "church as usual." Transform our thinking. Transform our living. And please, Lord, use us as Your partners to help transform this world that You love so much, until that day when the whole world will sing Your praises. In Jesus' name, Amen.

Transformed Thinking

Read: When you hear the word *church*, what are the first images that come to mind? We often picture buildings, clergy, choirs, worship leaders, programs and members. During Jesus' time on earth, however, *ekklesia*—the Greek word most often translated into English as *church*—was not religious in connotation at all. The *ekklesia* was a secular institution operating in the marketplace in a governmental capacity. As you are already discovering in your reading of *Ekklesia*, Jesus co-opted this secular institution and impregnated it with Kingdom DNA. In the process, He introduced and launched a "radical proposition"—His Church, His Ekklesia.

As you read in chapter 1, back in New Testament times *church* always referred to people, never to buildings. The early Church operated "from house to house" as a transforming organism, not as a static institution. Its object was the transformation of people and society; it was not acting as "a transfer station for saved souls bound for heaven."

The rapid growth of the first-century Ekklesia began on the Day of Pentecost, when three thousand believed and were baptized. The message of salvation and new life through Jesus Christ spread like wildfire. After just a few years, what began in Jerusalem had expanded so much that Luke reported in the book of Acts that "all who lived in Asia heard the word of the Lord, both Jews and Greeks" (Acts 19:10). Churches were planted, leaders were chosen and whole cities and regions felt the impact in rapid succession. From the very beginning, Jesus' Ekklesia could not be contained within four walls.

As I said in the book, this stunningly remarkable accomplishment took place without military or governmental support. It was instead "a massive *people movement* that swept region after region victoriously as the counterculture to the existing status quo." And, "it was so healthy and powerful that rather than being an item on someone else's agenda, the Ekklesia was the agenda setter!"

Share: What are some aspects of "being the Church" today that we need to rediscover in order to be the agenda setters in transforming both people and society?

_____

_____

_____

Read: During Jesus' 33 years on earth, three major institutions shaped the life of the Jewish people: the Temple, the synagogue and the ekklesia. The first two were religious. The third was secular.

- Built on the highest hill in Jerusalem, the Temple was central to the life of the Jewish nation. In obedience to the Torah—the books of the Law—the Temple was the focal point of ritual animal sacrifices, as well as the location of religious ceremonies and festivals at which thousands of pilgrims gathered every year.
- The synagogue was similar to a local congregation today. It was the place that Jews met on the Sabbath—Saturday—to read the Scriptures, receive teaching and pray. The Hebrew word translated *synagogue* literally means "a house of prayer." The synagogue also served as a connecting point for fellowship and Jewish community life.

- The ekklesia was a secular institution first developed in the Greek city-states, where duly appointed citizens were given authority to legislate on local matters in the public square. Later, when the Romans replaced the Greeks on the world scene, the ekklesia also served to infuse newly conquered territories with the culture and customs of Rome. In addition, when two or three Roman citizens gathered concerning the interests of the empire, the power and authority of the emperor was in their midst. This smaller gathering was called the *Conventus Civium Romanorum*, or *conventus* for short.

When Jesus launched His "transformational agency," He did not choose the Temple or the synagogue. Instead, He chose to co-opt and impregnate a secular institution, the ekklesia, with Kingdom DNA. This statement I made in chapter 1 covers the key distinctions between the Temple, the synagogue and Jesus' Ekklesia:

The Temple and the synagogue were static institutions that functioned in buildings that members had to go to on specified occasions, whereas the Ekklesia was a *building-less* mobile people movement designed to operate 24/7 in the marketplace for the purpose of having an impact on everybody and everything.

Share: In your view, which of these first-century institutions—the Temple, the synagogue or Jesus' Ekklesia—does the Church of today most reflect? What positive qualities are incorporated from each? What is missing?

_____

_____

_____

_____

Read: In the same way that Rome decreed through the secular ekklesia that wherever two or three Roman citizens gathered, the presence and authority of Rome was there, Jesus promised His presence and authority to the "citizens of His Kingdom" in an even greater dimension. In Matthew 18:18–20 Jesus declared:

Truly I say to you, whatever you bind on earth shall have been bound in heaven; and whatever you loose on earth shall have been loosed in heaven.

Again I say to you, that if two of you agree on earth about anything that they may ask, it shall be done for them by My Father who is in heaven. For where two or three have gathered together in My name, I am there in their midst.

Share: Not discounting the authority given to us as individual Christians, what is the quorum described here for believers who are praying in agreement to experience Jesus' presence and power as a microscopic expression of His Ekklesia?

In what ways is this "low threshold" for a quorum an encouragement to the Ekklesia today?

Deeper: What are some examples of things that we, as Jesus' disciples and members of His Ekklesia, have the authority to bind and to loose? What can hold us back from claiming these promises and exercising this privilege?

Read: By injecting "Kingdom DNA" into a well-known secular institution, Jesus was also able to co-opt other important social tracks, for example, meals. We might say that in doing likewise, the early Church moved from the Temple to the kitchen table. In Acts 2:42, for example, the first believers were seen "continually devoting themselves to the apostles' teaching and to fellowship, to the breaking of bread [eating] and to prayer."

I comment in the book that one of the most common examples of an early Church meeting involved believers partaking of both food and the doctrine of the apostles. Those shared mealtimes inserted the Ekklesia into everyday life, which had the effect of turning tables into pulpits and homes into assembly halls "into which strangers were welcome, rendering them prime candidates for evangelism."

Share: How are mealtimes used in your culture within families, among friends, for business purposes or to foster new or growing relationships?

As a member of Jesus' Ekklesia today, how can you leverage meals as an already existing social track through which you can reach people for Christ who are not believers yet?

Deeper: Recall some special social times that Jesus shared with others. How did these moments lead to transformed lives? (Think about the example of Zaccheus.)

_____

_____

Session Summary

- Jesus' Ekklesia is a dynamic *people movement* rather than a rigid, static organization. It is meant to be centered in the marketplace, not in buildings.
- By the *marketplace* we mean the combination of business, education and government that constitutes the arteries through which the life of a city and a nation flow daily.
- Jesus chose the ekklesia model over the Temple or the synagogue because it could serve more effectively as a mobile people movement operating 24/7 for the purpose of transforming society and its culture globally.
- A key element in the life of the early Ekklesia was the sharing of meals, along with the apostles' teaching. This social track became an opportunity to welcome nonbelievers and introduce them to Jesus in a friendly setting, something we should continue to do today.
- Our commitment as an eGroup is to discover the deeper meaning and application of Jesus' Ekklesia so that nations will be discipled, starting right where we are.

Transformed Living

Read: The key to rediscovering the deeper truth regarding Jesus' Ekklesia is to *apply* what we are learning to everyday life, relying fully on the power of the Holy Spirit and expecting God to perform miracles through us. Therefore, I encourage you to accept the **Personal Life Application** and the **Group Life Application** that I present in this **Transformed Living** section near the end of every session. You can complete some of the applications during the upcoming week. Other applications will continue for several weeks, and as appropriate, well into the future. Transformation is a lifestyle, not a program, and it starts in us. With firm resolve, and with total dependence on the grace of God, the love of Jesus and the power of the Holy Spirit, you will become a dynamic member in Jesus' Ekklesia!

Prayer evangelism represents a biblical lifestyle you will be hearing a great deal about in the sessions ahead. It is the evangelistic method that Jesus taught His disciples, as recorded in the gospels, and it is detailed in Luke 10:1–18. In a single phrase, prayer evangelism is *"talking to God about your neighbors before you talk to your neighbors about God."* When we direct our prayers outside the walls of the Church, they become the vehicle for evangelism—prayer evangelism.

By way of simple introduction, this four-step strategy that Jesus taught is the key to first having an impact on, and then eventually transforming, the marketplace. You will see this strategy illustrated in many riveting examples in my book as you move through this study. Here are the four steps:

- *Bless* the lost and speak peace to them (see Luke 10:5).
- *Fellowship* with them, eating and drinking together (see verse 7).
- *Minister* to them, taking care of their needs and praying for miracles (see verse 9).
- *Proclaim* "the kingdom of God has come near to you" (verse 9).

You will discover that the tipping point in this strategy is step 3, ministering to the lost. As you minister to them, first responding to their felt needs in tangible ways, you will also be offering prayers of faith for miracles, especially for those people who don't yet know Jesus. Miracles should become the norm, not the exception. The source for the miraculous will become clearer to you once we cover the chapters in *Ekklesia* about the Holy Spirit.

The first step of prayer evangelism, however, is blessing the lost and speaking peace to them, so let's start there. Your first **Personal Life Application** is to "bless and speak peace" to those people in your sphere of influence—your family, neighborhood, workplace or school.

You may find this challenging at first, but remember that this is God's idea. He will empower you to carry it out. Ask Him to help you. Remember that when you "bless and speak peace," you are not necessarily agreeing with everything that you see going on in people's lives. Rather, you are expressing a heartfelt desire that they would come to experience God's presence and power. Your first opportunities to "bless and speak peace" may come as you take the dog for a walk or as you open the door to your office or factory and begin a new workweek. Begin by declaring blessings and peace first in your silent prayers, and then in more tangible ways as you follow the leading of the Holy Spirit. Dr. Greg Pagh, my partner in this curriculum project, writes,

> I experienced a significant shift in my attitude years ago, when I began to "bless and speak peace" to those around me. Even while driving my car, what formerly had been "drive-by curses" turned into "drive-by blessings," and in the process, I began to see the people and places around me through a different lens, the way God sees them.

Be prepared to share your experience of blessing and speaking peace to others with your eGroup at the beginning of the next session.

Your **Group Life Application** is twofold. First, pray daily by name for every person in your eGroup during the coming week. Also bless and speak peace to them, reinforcing the first step of prayer evangelism. Part of your commitment to your group is to pray for one another. As you pray for your fellow group members, you will also be learning their names so that you can greet them by name at your next session, or should you see them between meetings. The relationships that you build in your eGroup are foundational to the relationships you will be asked to build beyond your group.

Second, plan a meal hosted by your eGroup and invite others to join you who would be blessed by an opportunity to make some new friends (perhaps a neighbor, a co-worker, a classmate or others). This meal could take place in one of your homes, at a local restaurant, in a coffee shop or at a public park. Schedule it at a different time from your upcoming group sessions.

This opportunity relates to the fact that a key element in the growth of the early Ekklesia was the sharing of meals, along with the apostles' teaching. This social track will not only help relationships grow deeper in your eGroup, but will also become an avenue for reaching out to others in a nonthreatening way.

The key is to insert the leaven of the Ekklesia into something that is part of everyday life—meals. If you meet at a restaurant, gather in the parking lot before you go in and pray for the owner and staff. If you meet in a home, bless that home and neighborhood and invite the presence of the Lord to fill that place. Encourage each other to share a testimony or a Scripture that has really had an impact on your lives. Lead by "blessing and speaking peace."

Talk about this group application now. Pick a date, time and place. Who will be the point person to coordinate the details and group communications? Whom else will you invite? Develop your plan of action and have fun while practicing how to emulate the Ekklesia in Jerusalem, as reported in Acts 2:42.

_____

_____

_____

_____

Ekklesia Prayer and Ministry

Every week you will be encouraged to take a few minutes to share personal prayer requests for yourself, your family and others with your eGroup. Your group meeting will close with a time of prayer and ministry to one another.

Endeavor to pray prayers of faith. These are prayers that claim the promises found in God's Word, as led by the Holy Spirit (see James 5:13–18). You can write your requests and those of others in your group down here to help you remember them:

_____

_____

_____

_____

_____

Reading Assignment

In preparation for Session 2, read chapter 2 in my book *Ekklesia*, entitled "Transformation Is a Journey."

Daily Devotions

Read: It is important for your Christian growth as a member of the Ekklesia that you cultivate a daily discipline of personal Bible reading, reflection, listening to the Holy Spirit and intercessory prayer. Below you will find some passages of Scripture, followed by questions for reflection that further connect with the topics from this week's session.

I encourage you to establish a time for these daily devotions that is workable with your lifestyle. Begin your devotional time with prayer. Ask the Holy Spirit to illuminate your reading of God's Word, quickening your mind to listen to His leading. Read the suggested Scripture passages more than once. Reflect on the questions provided and other questions that will come to your mind. Consider the applications to your daily life, and envision how to carry them out.

Then take a longer time to pray. Let the Holy Spirit lead you to higher and deeper levels of prayer (see Romans 8:26–27). Come before the Lord with confession, praise and thanksgiving. Pray for the needs in your personal life, family and church, but also in your community, since that is where the Ekklesia is meant to operate 24/7. Take time to listen, too. Psalm 46:10 says, "Cease striving and know that I am God."

The time frame for these daily devotions may grow from 10–15 minutes to an hour or more as your devotional life deepens. Be encouraged by the fact that other members of your eGroup have committed to praying for you during this journey. Do Day One's devotion the first day after your group meeting, and follow the devotions day by day right through the week until Day Seven, when your group meets again.

Day One—Luke 10:1–24

Have you been on a mission trip to serve beyond your local area, perhaps even in a different country? Review the instructions Jesus gave His disciples as He sent them on a mission trip "to every city and place where He Himself was going to come" (verse 1). Why are these instructions still vital to our witness to the world today? Why did the disciples return with joy (see verse 17)? Why does verse 21 of today's Scripture say that Jesus "rejoiced greatly in the Holy Spirit"?

Day Two—Matthew 28:16–20

The Great Commission, as this Scripture passage is called, represents Jesus' final marching orders to His disciples as He prepared to ascend into heaven to ask the Father to send the Holy Spirit and empower the disciples to preach the Gospel and disciple nations (see also Mark 16:15). As we "go" throughout our daily life, what are we to do? What does Jesus promise to do?

Day Three—Colossians 3:12–25

Which of the Christlike qualities described in verses 12–14 as "clothing" do you most need to adorn your life today? Reflect on an aspect of your life where you need to "let the peace of Christ rule" in your heart (verse 15). Which of the instructions verses 18–21 give to families will contribute the most right now to strengthening your family? How could you bring greater excellence to your daily work (see verse 23)?

Day Four—Acts 18:1–11

Reflect on times when you have reached outside the walls of your local church to be a witness in the marketplace (in the areas of business, education or government). What happened? Did you face some opposition, or even persecution? How did Jesus speak words of reassurance to you, as He did to Paul in verses 9–10 of today's Scripture? Did you experience breakthroughs? How did that affect you?

Day Five—Revelation 21:22–27

Picture in your mind the Olympic opening ceremonies, as athletes participate in the parade of nations in anticipation of this global sports competition. Now imagine "discipled nations" and their leaders coming before the Lord, bringing the restored glory and honor of their nations as a wedding present to Jesus. This is the ultimate mission of Jesus' Ekklesia. Reflect further on today's Scripture and thank God that you are called to be part of this process to rediscover Jesus' Ekklesia.

Day Six—Ephesians 3:14–21

In what ways are you "being rooted and grounded in love" (verse 17)? Is your heart truly open to being "filled up to all the fullness of God" (verse 19)? During your prayer time today, ask Jesus "to do far more abundantly beyond all that we [you] ask or think," according to His power that is at work within you (verse 20) so that the Ekklesia may glorify Jesus throughout all generations, including the present one.

Day Seven—your eGroup meets today!

SESSION 2

Transformation is a process. Like the feeble light at the crack of dawn, it is meant to grow brighter and brighter. But the "dawn" does not happen, and the path remains untraveled, until one begins taking steps of obedience in the right direction.

You will embark on your own exciting journey to rediscover the Church as Jesus really meant it to be, and to discover in the Scriptures what we have missed in the current expression of the Church, so that the powerful and life-changing things that customarily take place inside its four walls will also happen through you in the public square. You will never be the same. You will come to love weekdays as much as you already love Sundays, once you get going on this transformation journey.

Sharing Life

Watch: Play the video introduction for Session 2. This session is based on chapter 2 in my *Ekklesia* book, "Transformation Is a Journey."

Pray Together: Dear heavenly Father, thank You for bringing our Ekklesia group back together today. Thank You for the opportunity to grow as brothers and sisters in Christ. Thank You for Jesus, our Savior, who gave His life that we might have abundant and eternal life, and who rose from the dead and now lives in us. Thank You for the Holy Spirit, who is assigned to lead us to all truth and righteousness. Thank You for Your Word, which is the firm foundation upon which we are committed to build our lives. Please come and preside among us now. Illuminate our study with deep insights. Guide us by the Holy Spirit as we share, so that Your true Ekklesia will be manifested in all we say and do. In Jesus' all-powerful name we pray, Amen.

Read: Begin this session by reviewing your **Life Applications** from Session 1.

Share: Your first **Personal Life Application** was to "bless and speak peace" to those in your sphere of influence: your family, neighborhood, workplace, school or local church. Did you do it? What did you experience? Who was the hardest to bless? What did God do in your heart?

Your **Group Life Application** was twofold. First, you were to pray by name for those in your eGroup, "bless and speak peace to them" and learn their names. Second, you were to plan an eGroup meal in order to build relationships and reach out to others. What did you plan? Whom did you invite? Where was your meal held? How did it go? What did God teach you?

If your group meal has not taken place yet, are there details that you still need to finalize? The key is to insert the "leaven" of the Ekklesia into something that is a part of everyday life, like meals. The goal is to model for others the love and kindness of Jesus, which always looks outward to be a blessing to others.

Read: Remember, the **Life Applications** are meant to build on one another each week and lead to a transformational lifestyle, because as members of Jesus' Ekklesia we are all called to "disciple nations." That starts right where we are, in our families, workplaces, churches and communities.

Transformed Thinking

Read: Proverbs 4:18 says, "The path of the righteous is like the light of dawn, that shines brighter and brighter until the full day." I begin chapter 2 in *Ekklesia* with a foundational statement that sets the direction for the rest of the book: "Transformation is a process that shifts paradigms so that we can see what we have not seen before, which allows us to do what we have not done yet. And for this, we must be open to change."

A paradigm is a framework for perceiving and understanding the world around us. A paradigm shift takes place when we are led to "believe, think and act" in a new way because we have gained knowledge or insights that we did not previously have.

Share: Identify one major paradigm shift that took place in your life as a result of coming to know Jesus Christ as your Savior and Lord. In other words, what has changed about the way you "believe, think and act" because you are now a follower of Jesus?

_____

_____

Read: In chapter 2 of the book, I recount our family and ministry's global transformation journey from a prayer chapel in Argentina to every continent on earth. This journey of "rediscovering God's instrument for global transformation" began for me at age 34, when my doctors told me I had a maximum of two years to live. Motivated to serve God to the fullest with whatever time remained in my life, Ruth and I leveraged our limited resources to build a prayer chapel in our beloved Argentina, where there were no evangelical churches at that time in any of the 109 towns within a 100-mile radius.

God healed me, and today, as a testimony to the fact that we should never despise small beginnings, every one of those towns has been evangelized. There are many evangelical churches and leaders in those places who honor us as "spiritual parents." God has continued to open doors for us around the world, so that we can go and inspire others to embrace a transformation lifestyle. Prototypes have been developed that have resulted in powerful testimonies and important insights as the timeless truths of the Bible have been applied in the most challenging of circumstances, and as a result, a global movement is now touching people and nations all over the world.

In addition to *Ekklesia*, I have authored five previous books that I briefly describe in chapter 2. Each book summarizes key steps in this lifelong transformation journey, so they are foundational to our study of Jesus' Ekklesia. I encourage you to read my other books to learn more about the transformation process. But for the purpose of our study here, I am including a short summary of what each book contributed to the transformation movement, along with some questions for your group discussion. (You can find the publisher and year for each of these books in chapter 2's end notes in *Ekklesia*.)

That None Should Perish

- You can reach an entire city through prayer evangelism. As a result, the Church can experience extraordinary growth. The city of Resistencia, Argentina, with a population 400,000, became "the proof of concept" for this when the evangelical population grew from 5,143 to over 11,000 in the first year of applying prayer evangelism. Today, the number of believers in that city has surpassed 100,000, with many more in the region who are reportedly born again.

Prayer Evangelism

- Prayer and evangelism are two sides of the same coin.
- It is possible to change the spiritual climate over a city and a region.
- It is biblical to meet the felt needs of unbelievers without demanding that they first receive Christ. The main objective of this approach is to put them in touch with God through answered prayer, so that they are drawn to Him.
- I call the four-step strategy Jesus taught His disciples in Luke 10 *prayer evangelism* because prayer becomes evangelism when we focus it on the felt needs of lost people, cities and nations. Here are the four steps of prayer evangelism again:

1. *Bless* the lost and speak peace to them (see Luke 10:5).
2. *Fellowship* with them, eating and drinking together (see verse 7).
3. *Minister* to them, taking care of their needs and praying for miracles (see verse 9).
4. *Proclaim* "the kingdom of God has come near to you" (see verse 9).

The immediate result of this four-step "Jesus strategy" is that it changes the spiritual climate, as it did in Luke 10, because Satan falls down and his demons become subject to Jesus' Ekklesia, and multitudes enthusiastically come into the Kingdom (see Luke 10:17–18; 16:16).

Share: How would you assess the current spiritual climate in your city or region?

_____

_____

Why is the order of prayer evangelism's four steps important regarding how it impacts and changes us? Why is the order important when it comes to how the message of Christ is ultimately received?

_____

_____

Women—God's Secret Weapon
- Men and women are designed and empowered to honor one another and walk in harmony in order to reflect God's image first in the home, and then in the city and beyond.
- Women have a legitimate and important role in ministry.
- Without gender reconciliation—beginning with husbands and wives—prayers will be hindered, especially those of husbands. (See 1 Peter 3:7.)

Share: In chapter 2 I quote missionary C. T. Studd as saying, "The light that shines farthest shines brightest at home." What does this mean to you?

_____

_____

Anointed for Business
- Every believer is a minister.
- Pastors are called to train, equip and release members to be ministers in the marketplace every day.

- Marketplace ministry is not a program in the Church, but a daily ministry in the marketplace in the arenas of business, education and government, which comprise every area of society.
- Pulpit and marketplace ministers must work as full partners in order to see cities and nations transformed.

Share: What has been implied in the Church through the use of terms such as *laypeople* and *clergy*? Are these biblical terms?

_____

_____

_____

Deeper: Why does this terminology run counter to our preliminary understanding of Jesus' Ekklesia?

_____

_____

_____

Transformation
- Five pivotal paradigms of nation transformation express biblical truths that the Church has often ignored, misunderstood or misapplied. As we embrace these pivotal paradigms, paradigm shifts will take place that lead us as the Ekklesia to believe, think and act as Jesus did. Here are the five pivotal paradigms, which I list in chapter 2 and discuss in more detail in chapter 16 of *Ekklesia*:
  1. The Great Commission is about discipling nations and not just individuals (see Matthew 28:19).
  2. The Atonement secured redemption not only for individuals, but also for the marketplace, which is the heart of the nation (see Luke 19:10).
  3. Labor is worship, and since all believers are ministers, they are to turn their jobs into places of worship to God and ministry to others (see Colossians 3:23).
  4. Jesus is the One who builds His Church, not us. Our assignment is to use the keys of the Kingdom to lock and unlock the Gates of Hades in order for Him to build His Church where those Gates stand (see Matthew 16:19).
  5. The elimination of systemic poverty in its four dimensions— spiritual, relational, motivational and material—is the premier tangible social indicator of transformation (see Luke 4:18).

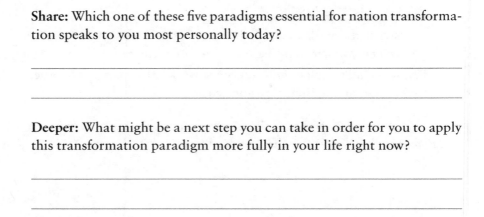

Share: Which one of these five paradigms essential for nation transformation speaks to you most personally today?

_____

_____

Deeper: What might be a next step you can take in order for you to apply this transformation paradigm more fully in your life right now?

_____

_____

Read: As I say at the end of chapter 2, the purpose of my journey in writing _Ekklesia_ was to rediscover the Church as Jesus _really_ meant it to be, and to search the Scriptures to look for what we have missed in our current expression of the Church, so that the powerful and life-changing things that customarily take place inside the Church's four walls also will happen in the public square. Likewise, that is the purpose of our journey together throughout this study, and the results will be exciting and revolutionary both in your life and the lives of those around you.

Session Summary

- The transformation journey is a process that requires that we shift paradigms to be able to see what we never saw before.
- In order to rediscover the real Church Jesus is building, which is God's instrument for global transformation, we must embrace the original teaching of Jesus regarding the Ekklesia in both word and deed.
- Because prayer is foundational to transformation, prayer evangelism must become a lifestyle, not just another program.
- In Jesus' Ekklesia, the same life-changing experiences that have traditionally happened within the four walls of a church building will also happen in the public square.

Transformed Living

Read: The second step of prayer evangelism is _fellowship_. In order to build relationships with the unsaved in our spheres of influence, we must find natural ways to connect in the context of everyday life. As we have already seen, when we "bless and speak peace" to the lost, the spiritual climate begins to change. Speaking peace to "whatever house you enter" opens the door of that "house" to authentic fellowship, from which relationships can develop. We must build trust with unbelievers, because they may start out with the assumption that we don't like them and are standing in judgment of their lives. As we reveal ourselves to others, they are more likely to open up to us. Don't be concerned about ministering or preaching to them yet. Be patient with the process. We are all on a transformation journey.

Your **Personal Life Application** this week has two parts. First, continue to "bless and speak peace" to those in your spheres of influence, asking God to open doors to fellowship with them. Second, in order to practice building relationships with unsaved people, share a cup of coffee or a meal with a neighbor, a classmate or a co-worker over whose life or house you have been speaking peace and blessing. Step out in faith and choose someone whom you don't know that well yet. This opportunity will help you get to know the person better, and you will be able to continue practicing the principles of prayer evangelism as a lifestyle as you follow these steps that build one upon the other.

Be loving and practical in your approach. The premise of your invitation is simply, "I'd like to get to know you better." Listen at least as much as you talk. Pay for the coffee or meal. Remember Jesus' promise in Matthew 18:20: "Where two or three have gathered together in My name, I am there in their midst." Invite the Holy Spirit to be present with you, guiding your conversation. Begin to listen for the felt needs of the person, which are the most obvious, pressing needs in his or her life.

Your **Group Life Application** builds on the group application from Session 1, which was to share in an eGroup meal and invite others to join you. If you have not yet been able to schedule this fellowship opportunity, make every effort to make it happen this week.

If you have already had your "a la Acts 2:42" group meal, here is your next assignment to build on the fellowship you have already enjoyed: Follow up with at least one of your guests at the meal with a friendly and encouraging phone call, email or text, as seems appropriate. You may be surprised at how significant this kind of encouragement can be in someone's life, especially to those who don't yet know the Lord. This "electronic connection" may lead to another opportunity to meet personally and share life together. You can note your follow-up contacts here:

_____

_____

_____

_____

Next week, you may be asked in your eGroup to report on one of your contacts. (Note: Be very discerning and discreet about sharing personal information or confidential matters when you report back to your group.)

Ekklesia Prayer and Ministry

Take a few minutes to share personal prayer requests for yourself and others, or situations in your workplace, school or community that are on your heart. And most importantly, don't limit this exercise to just sharing prayer requests. As time allows, close with a period of Spirit-led prayer and ministry to one another. Include prayers for boldness to reach out to others this coming week. This prayer and ministry time may be the most important part of your eGroup session together. Offer prayers of faith as a group. Prayers of faith are prayers rooted in God's promises, offered in the power and leading of the Holy Spirit, with an expectation of divine intervention in whichever way God chooses to respond. You can jot down the prayer requests here to help you remember them:

_____

_____

_____

_____

_____

Reading Assignment

In preparation for Session 3, read chapter 3 in *Ekklesia*, "A Fuller Understanding of the Gates of Hades."

Daily Devotions

Read: I encourage you to build on your devotional discipline from Session 1. Ask the Lord to help you overcome obstacles that may have kept you from cultivating a daily routine of Bible reading, reflection and prayer. Below, you will again find some passages of Scripture for each day of the coming week, starting with Day One tomorrow. Each day, read the Bible passage, reflect on the questions and pray as God leads you. Strive to be obedient to the direction of the Holy Spirit. Be blessed!

Day One—Psalm 118:19–29

How has God answered you and become your salvation? If you began every day by declaring verse 24 from this psalm, how would it change your attitude? How would it help you appreciate every day as a gift from God? How would it help you bless and speak peace to others?

Day Two—John 1:35–51

How did Jesus' core group of disciples grow? Whom might you invite to "come and see," as Jesus invited the men in verse 39? Why have you chosen to follow Jesus? Reread verse 51. Have the heavens opened for you lately? What has God been showing you?

Day Three—Romans 12:9–18

Which qualities described in this passage of Scripture do you consider the most important in building strong relationships with others? What is one of your favorite ways of practicing hospitality? Why do real friends both rejoice and weep with one another?

Day Four—John 4:1–26

How did Jesus use a felt need to connect to a deeper need in the life of the woman at the well? How did Jesus turn their conversation from religion to relationship? Where are the "watering holes" in your daily life, where you can find opportunities to share in conversations and respond to the needs of others?

Day Five—Philippians 4:10–20

What is the secret of being content in every situation? Is there a situation in your life right now where you really need the strength of the Lord the way verse 13 talks about? Be reassured and encouraged that "God will supply all your needs according to His riches in glory in Christ Jesus" (verse 19).

Day Six—Galatians 5:13–15

What is the difference between serving out of love and serving out of duty, both for the one serving and for the one being served? Reflect on some practical examples of how you can "love your neighbor as yourself" (verse 14). Have you ever been consumed by anger (see verse 15)? This passage encourages you to let it go because Jesus has called you to freedom, and consuming anger has serious consequences.

Day Seven—your eGroup meets today!

SESSION 3

Light dispels darkness, which is exactly why Jesus defined the function of His Ekklesia as an operation of light against the spiritual darkness covering the world. He associated darkness with the Gates of Hades, and made reference to the fact that His Ekklesia would prevail against those gates—something that the book of Acts chronicles in a manner that provides faith and inspiration for us to believe that we can overcome evil today. For the Church today to emulate the book of Acts in that regard, it must relearn the spiritual dimension of life in order to confront and defeat the demonic entrenchment in both the heavenlies and on earth.

What you will walk away with:

You will have a renewed understanding of the spiritual dimension of life that will empower you to confront and defeat the entrenchment of the Gates of Hades in both the heavenlies and on earth, particularly in areas that are impacting your sphere of influence. In essence, you will learn how to switch from a POW camp to a Marine mindset, so that the will of God can be done on earth, as it is already done in heaven.

Sharing Life

Watch: Play the video introduction for Session 3. This session is based on chapter 3 in *Ekklesia*, "A Fuller Understanding of the Gates of Hades."

Pray Together: Dear Jesus, Thank You that You have promised to be with us always. Thank You that as our Ekklesia group gathers again today, You are right here with us. Open our minds to "think outside the box." Help us never settle for comfortable traditions, when You desire to fill us with greater vision for the sake of building Your Kingdom here on earth. Show us today how to access Your wisdom and power, to see Your will done in our lives and in our spheres of influence, so that the Gates of Hades will not prevail, but will be defeated. In Jesus' almighty and precious name we pray, Amen.

Read: Begin this session by reviewing your **Life Applications** from Session 2.

Share: Your **Personal Life Application** this past week was to invite a neighbor, co-worker or classmate for whom you have been praying and speaking peace to join you for a cup of coffee or a meal in order to develop your relationship and begin to discern the person's felt needs. Whom did you meet with? What did you do? How did the conversation go? Reflect on your application of the first two steps of prayer evangelism, which are to "bless and speak peace" and to "fellowship" or build relationships with those who don't yet know Jesus. What did the Holy Spirit reveal to you?

Your **Group Life Application** this past week was either to complete the group meal opportunity presented during Session 1 or to follow up with the guests you invited to attend the group meal, contacting them with a friendly and encouraging phone call, text or email.

Where is your group at with this application? Did you share together in the group meal this week? What did you do? Who was invited? How did it go? Did the Holy Spirit use this opportunity to help you fellowship with others as the second step of prayer evangelism? Did any of your conversations lead to spiritual topics or open the door so you could share part of your testimony?

_____

_____

_____

_____

For those who did the follow-up contacts, how were they received? Did technology provide another "social track" for you to run on? How were your texts, emails or phone calls received? What is God teaching you about building relationships with those who don't yet know Jesus?

_____

_____

_____

_____

Transformed Thinking

Read: One key success factor in the phenomenal growth of the Ekklesia in the New Testament was its thorough understanding of the nature and operation of what Jesus called the "Gates of Hades." When Jesus launched

His agency of transformation, He declared, "I will build My church [Ekklesia]; and the gates of Hades will not overpower it" (Matthew 16:18).

What are the Gates of Hades, and how is the Church to defeat them? In chapter 3 of *Ekklesia* you read that the Gates of Hades represent Satan's evil domain run by spiritual deputies who are entrenched in the heavenly places to control specific segments of society on earth. In Ephesians 6:12, the apostle Paul highlights this dual dimension of evil presence when he acknowledges that we struggle against "the rulers, against the powers, against the *world* forces of this darkness, against the spiritual forces of wickedness in the *heavenly* places" (emphasis added). As you can see, the evil forces Jesus described as the Gates of Hades operate in both the "worldly" and "heavenly" realms. In chapter 3 of the book, I make this statement:

> Terms such as *spiritual forces* and *heavenly places* can easily mislead us to conclude that it is an ethereal reign. But the overriding context in the book of Ephesians, where this teaching is found, is that it is the Ekklesia's mission to heal unreconciled *human* realities that exist in the *earthly realm*. Ephesians talks about ethnic divisions in chapter 2, religious disunity in chapter 3, ministerial competition in chapter 4, discord between genders in chapter 5, and family strife and marketplace injustice in chapter 6.
>
> These social gaps reflect how the spirit realm determines the state of affairs on earth . . .

Share: From your perspective, which of the following six unreconciled social gaps most directly represents the Gates of Hades operating in your city or region? Explain why.

- Ethnic division
- Religious disunity
- Ministerial competition
- Discord between genders
- Family strife
- Marketplace injustice

_____

_____

_____

Read: We cannot confront and defeat the Gates of Hades until we recognize both the *eternal* and *temporal* dimensions of our battle. Too often, our eyes are blinded by human reason, pride or ignorance. Thus, when observing the myriad manifestations of evil in our world, our first instinct is to shrink back in fear rather than confronting evil by claiming and appropriating the victory Jesus assured us of. As a result, the contemporary Church, generally speaking, looks so much weaker compared to what we read about the Ekklesia in the book of Acts. In my discovery journey, I often felt as if I were walking through a minefield. This was because what I saw in the Scriptures about the Ekklesia was not only different from, but too often at odds with, what we call the "Church" today.

When and why did we go wrong? In the book chapter for this session, I introduced two significant *negative* historical factors that have undermined the true meaning of the Ekklesia and that require us to take a second look in order to rediscover the Church that Jesus is building today. These factors can be summarized as the centralized control of the Church, and power and politics. You can read about them in more detail in *Ekklesia* itself, but let's take a brief look at each here.

Centralized control of the Church: Roman emperors from Constantine to Charlemagne, along with many other world leaders since, have fostered centralized control of the Church by developing close alliances between their governments and the organized Church. Bishops and popes were controlled by emperors and kings, and vice versa. These intertwined relationships negatively affected the growth and health of the Ekklesia. As I state in chapter 3, "This illicit marriage of the eternal with the temporal has always arrested the intended impact of the Ekklesia, because . . . the latter is meant to be expansive, like salt, water, light or leaven."

Power and politics: In the sixteen hundreds, King James of England created his King James "Authorized" Version of the Bible. Under penalty of death, his appointed scholars had to translate the Greek word *ekklesia* as "church" rather than "assembly." Why? To perpetuate the king's belief in the "divine right of kings" to rule with absolute authority, not allowing any room for local congregations or individual Christians to express their views or follow the leading of the Holy Spirit. His intention was to keep the government of the Church in his hands. As I state in the book, "Etymologically speaking, *church* means 'of the Lord,' but it was the wrong translation for the Greek word *ekklesia*. To make matters worse, by that time the word *church* had been defined and was perceived as a building with clergy."

Share: In light of the historical insights here and detailed in chapter 3, how might it change your perspective if the word *ekklesia* were translated in your Bible as "assembly" or "congregation" rather than "church?"

_____

_____

Deeper: How would you describe the current dynamic between the Christian Church and the government in your country? Partnerships? Points of tension? Freedom or oppression?

_____

_____

Read: In spite of these historical setbacks, which have continued to negatively influence our understanding of "church" to this very day, there is reason to hope that we will rediscover what the original Ekklesia knew from the start—because Jesus stated that the Gates of Hades would not prevail against it. As I explained in the book, ever since Jesus' resurrection, when He proclaimed that He now held in His hands the keys of Hades and Death, all the devil has been left with is "gates." Jesus has given the members of His Ekklesia "the keys of the Kingdom" to lock and unlock, to bind and loose all over the earth! He declared,

> I will build My church [Ekklesia], and the gates of Hades will not prevail against it. And I will give you the keys of the kingdom of heaven, and whatever you bind on earth will be bound in heaven, and whatever you loose on earth will be loosed in heaven.
>
> Matthew 16:18–19 NKJV

Let me also restate what I said near the end of our textbook chapter:

> This struggle is real and ongoing, but the outcome is already predetermined—the Gates of Hades will not prevail. For this, the Ekklesia must show up on the right field, the one where those Gates are entrenched. This is at the very center of the cry, "Your Kingdom come, *Your will be done on earth* as it is (already done) in heaven."

Share: Take the keys from your pocket or purse. How many do you have? Which keys are the most important: car, house, office, security box? What do these keys have in common?

_____

_____

Why is it important that we use "the keys of the Kingdom" that Jesus has given us? Why shouldn't we be intimidated by the size of the Gates of Hades?

_____

_____

_____

_____

Session Summary

- To overcome the Gates of Hades, we must first understand the dual dimension of evil, which includes spiritual battles in heavenly places and unreconciled human realities in the earthly realm.
- Historical factors and the Enlightenment have negatively distorted our understanding of the Church, making it necessary for us to re-discover the true Ekklesia as Jesus designed it to be, and as He is building it today, as evidenced by the case studies in the book.
- The Church belongs to Jesus, and He will build it, not us.
- We have been given "the keys of the Kingdom," and as a result we have authority to "bind evil" and "loose good" in Jesus' name.
- We can confront the Gates of Hades represented in society with confidence, because in Christ our victory is already assured, and as His Ekklesia we are deputized to reclaim everything that He redeemed.

Transformed Living

Read: The third step of prayer evangelism is to minister to the felt needs of the unsaved in Jesus' name and expect miracles. We minister in a variety of ways, including our presence, our prayers and through tangible acts of kindness. This is where our deeds must match our words.

As we are learning, when we "bless and speak peace," God opens doors to fellowship so that we can build relationships of trust. Jesus did not send His advance teams two-by-two to the synagogues, but rather to the homes and neighborhoods in the towns He was about to visit. We must meet people right where they are, in their homes, at work, at school, on the sports field and during times of joy and crisis.

As we not only talk to someone, but also become good listeners, the Holy Spirit will help us discern the felt need of that person. As we minister to the felt needs of others in Jesus' name, the Holy Spirit will open the door so we can also minister to their deeper needs. A felt need is the most current, pressing need that a person is experiencing. If someone is hungry, he or she wants food. If unemployed, the person needs a job. If marginalized, acceptance is the need. If someone is enslaved to sin, he or she needs a way out. If a city is experiencing violence, it needs peace. You get the idea.

Keep your eyes and your heart open. Keep speaking peace, and it will open doors for you. Keep fellowshiping and building relationships, until you identify the pain or sickness someone is dealing with. When you do that, minister to the person by offering prayer for God to meet that need, and expect a miracle. The Holy Spirit may prompt you to participate in that miracle as you respond in a tangible way with the gifts you have been given.

As we will learn in our next session, when God shows up, as He certainly will, we give Him all the credit and glory. At that point, we will be in a position to *proclaim* good news to people—that the God who has just come near to meet their need loves them and is available to them in the Person of Jesus Christ. *Proclaiming* is step 4 of the Spirit-led steps of prayer evangelism from Luke 10.

With the goal of continuing to develop a lifestyle related to the principles you are learning, your **Personal Life Application** during the coming week is to *continue to speak peace and build relationships with the people in your spheres of influence*. But now, begin to respond to the felt needs you have discerned with prayers of faith and action. Specifically, ask the Holy Spirit to give you an opportunity to pray for at least one person this week in response to a felt need, expecting a miracle. You can take notes to share with your eGroup next week:

_____

_____

_____

_____

Your **Group Life Application** this week is to see how many times you can use the phrase "the Kingdom of God has come near to you!"

Getting into the habit of connecting answers to prayer—especially answered prayers for others' needs—as an evidence of the presence of God and His Kingdom in the neighborhood is important for three reasons. First, it lets everyone know that as personal as the answer may have been, there is more awaiting them. "The Kingdom of God has come near" means that God is not finished; in fact, He has only begun.

Second, this phrase carries with it an echo that it is not just about you and your need; there is a Kingdom full of answers and resources for everyone and everything in your neighborhood, your city and eventually your nation.

Third, the phrase "the Kingdom of God has come near" is a prophetic declaration that becomes the word of your testimony, which is powerful in overcoming the evil one: "And they [believers] overcame him because of the blood of the Lamb and because of the word of their testimony, and they did not love their life even when faced with death" (Revelation 12:11). As a group, see how many times this week you have the opportunity to make the declaration "the Kingdom of God has come near to you!" in your spheres of influence. Record some of them here involving key people, events and encounters with God:

_____

_____

_____

_____

Ekklesia Prayer and Ministry

Take a few minutes to share personal prayer requests for yourself and others, or for situations in your church, business, school or community that are on your heart. Now, as time allows, close with a period of Spirit-led prayer and ministry to one another. Include prayers for wisdom and discernment regarding the social gap that your group will respond to as Jesus' Ekklesia in the weeks ahead. You can jot down the prayer requests here to help you remember them:

_____

_____

_____

_____

Reading Assignment

In preparation for Session 4, read chapters 4 and 5 of *Ekklesia*, "A Fuller Understanding of the Gospel" and "A Fuller Understanding of Proclamation." In addition, read all of Paul's letter to the Ephesians, noting the social gaps that he describes and the response he encourages from the early Ekklesia.

Daily Devotions

Read: How are you doing with your **Daily Devotions**? Are you setting aside a regular time each day or squeezing them in when you can? Don't give up! The more you are in the Word, the better equipped you will be to make a difference in the world. Below, you will again find some passages of Scripture for each day of the coming week, starting with Day One tomorrow. These passages build on the session you have just completed. Read the Scripture. Reflect on the questions. Pray as God leads you. Learn to listen to the Holy Spirit as He speaks to you, usually in the depth of your heart, or by planting or highlighting godly thoughts in your mind or bringing specific Bible passages into focus. Prayer is always a two-way street. Enjoy this special time with the Lord.

Day One—Jeremiah 31:31–34

What does God promise in the New Covenant? What do you think it means for God to write His law on our hearts? What does the statement in verse 33, "I will be their God, and they shall be My people," say about God's desire to have a relationship with you?

Day Two—John 17:13–26

Why didn't Jesus pray in verse 15 that God would take us out of the world? What does the word *sanctify* mean in verse 17? Why is unity a key to the Ekklesia's witness to the world (see verse 23)? In what ways can you "make Jesus known" this week (see verse 26)?

Day Three—1 Peter 2:4–10

Reflect on the differences in heart, attitude and actions between "living stones" in the Ekklesia and "dead stones." According to verse 9, why is God building us into a "spiritual house"?

Day Four—Titus 3:3–11

Contrast the life described in verse 3 with the life described in verses 5–7 after "the kindness of God our Savior and His love for mankind appeared" (verse 4). What an amazing transformation! These gifts from God allow us to engage in "good deeds" for the sake of the world.

Day Five—1 Corinthians 12:12–26

Why is it important for every person and part of the Body to work together in order for Jesus' Ekklesia to function properly? Who is the Head? What part of the Body of Christ are you? Have you learned to both appreciate your gifts and honor the gifts of others?

Day Six—2 Timothy 4:1–8

What does it mean in verse 2 to "preach the word; be ready in season and out of season"? Does this refer only to pastors, or to all who are part of the Ekklesia? How do people want their "ears tickled," as verse 3 says, today? What does it mean to you to "fulfill your ministry" (verse 5)? Every day? For a lifetime? Paul talks about his legacy in verses 7–8. What would you like your legacy to be?

Day Seven—your eGroup meets today! Enjoy!

SESSION 4

What this lesson is about:

In Luke 16:16, we learn that everyone was "forcing his way" into the Kingdom. In John 12:32, Jesus said, "And I, if I am lifted up from the earth, will draw all men to Myself." If Jesus is so irresistible and the Gospel is good news, could the refusal of people to receive it today be the result of our preaching something less? The biblical truths illuminated and highlighted in the chapters of *Ekklesia* we cover in this session constitute the theological tipping point for the Church as we know it today toward becoming the Ekklesia we read about in the New Testament.

What you will walk away with:

You will come away with a powerfully practical grasp on the Gospel of the Kingdom that changes everything in you, for you and around you. You will discover and learn how to experience the transforming presence of Jesus that the Ekklesia is called and empowered to take 24/7 to the marketplace so that multitudes are saved and cities are transformed. This discovery will propel you out of a passive "escapism" mindset and put you on a path of personal victory and transformation for yourself and for everything and everyone in your spheres of influence, as a prelude to what God plans to do in your city and beyond.

Sharing Life

Watch: Play the video introduction for Session 4. This session is based on chapters 4 and 5 in *Ekklesia*, "A Fuller Understanding of the Gospel" and "A Fuller Understanding of Proclamation."

Pray Together: Dear heavenly Father, thank You for each participant in our eGroup and our shared commitment to grow together in Christ and in the discovery of what His Ekklesia is meant to be. Thank You for opening our eyes to understand more of what Jesus had in mind when He launched the Ekklesia with the intent of transforming the world. As we begin this session, please help us embrace a fuller understanding of the Gospel of the Kingdom and the privilege we have to proclaim the "Good News" not just with words, but also with deeds. Help us learn that as members of the Ekklesia, we have been called to "right what is wrong" in people as well as in society, turning despair and misery into righteousness, peace and joy in the Holy Spirit. In Jesus' name, Amen.

Read: Begin this session by reviewing your **Life Application** from Session 3 together.

Share: Your **Personal Life Application** this past week was to continue steps 1 and 2 of prayer evangelism and to add step 3, which is to minister to the felt needs of the unsaved with prayers of faith and action, expecting miracles. You were asked to pray specifically with one of the people with whom you have been developing a relationship.

Did the Holy Spirit open an opportunity for this prayer to take place? What was the felt need you discerned? How did you pray? Was the person receptive? How is God answering this prayer? Have you received a miracle yet in the form of provision that could come only from God? Is God using you as part of this provision? Share your story!

Your **Group Life Application** was to see how many times this week you could use the phrase "the Kingdom of God has come near to you!" Take some time to share with the group what happened when you used it.

Transformed Thinking

Read: Chapter 4 of *Ekklesia* emphasizes that one of the most important keys to rediscovering the message of Jesus' Ekklesia is recognizing the difference between the "Law and the Prophets" and the "Gospel of the Kingdom." The Law and the Prophets focus on what God did in the past and what He has promised He will do in the future, whereas the Gospel of the Kingdom focuses on what Jesus can do *today*. This is a most important point to grasp in order for the Ekklesia message to become credible as it is validated by confirming signs emanating from Jesus' presence in its midst. Jesus signaled a shift in teaching that would become "the new normal" when He declared, "The Law and the Prophets were proclaimed until John; since that time the gospel of the kingdom of God has been preached, and everyone is forcing his way into it" (Luke 16:16).

Are people forcing their way into our Christian circles today with a hunger to come to Jesus and live their lives for Him? What keeps us from experiencing the extraordinary growth described in Luke 16:16, and what must we rediscover about Jesus' Ekklesia in order to reclaim what has been lost?

Here are some definitions from chapter 4 of the book to help you. The biblical phrase "the Law and the Prophets" refers to everything in the Old Testament that tells the story of God's relationship with the nation of Israel and His promise of a coming Savior. Its message, as I just stated, focuses primarily on what God *has done* in the past and what He *will do* in the future.

The "Gospel of the Kingdom of God," on the other hand, refers to everything in the New Testament, especially to Jesus' offer of salvation to the whole world as a result of His death and resurrection. This message focuses primarily on what God *can do and is determined to do in the present*. This shift in focus from the Law and the Prophets to a Gospel message that proclaims a "living Redeemer who is a present reality in our midst when as few as two or three gather in His name anywhere in the marketplace" resulted in phenomenal growth in the first-century Ekklesia, and it is a key issue for the Church today to rediscover. This is why I offered this caution in the book:

> When the Church as we know it today fails to make the transition from the Law and the Prophets to the Gospel of the Kingdom, it ends up preaching a message that is relevant to the past (Christ died on the cross to redeem us) and the future (He will return in glory), but it fails to present its relevance for today.

Share: Why do so many people today perceive the Church as irrelevant? Why is the message the Church is preaching not being more readily and enthusiastically received? Shouldn't people welcome the Good News?

_____

_____

_____

_____

Deeper: If you embrace and proclaim the teaching of the "Gospel of the Kingdom," that Jesus is present and active in our midst right now, how might this change how you worship, treat your family or do your job? And also, how should this affect everyone in your sphere of influence?

_____

_____

_____

_____

Read: Even though we are to proclaim enthusiastically the message of the Gospel of the Kingdom, the Good News of Jesus Christ, we must *avoid dichotomizing the Old and New Covenants* because it can lead to viewing the Jewish roots of the Gospel as irrelevant. It is more helpful when we see the Law and the Prophets (the Old) as the foundation upon which the Gospel of the Kingdom (the New) is built. We must avoid creating a stumbling block that will keep the Jewish people from hearing about the real Jesus today. As I say in chapter 4, "Everything taught in the Law and the Prophets points by direct reference, implication or inference to the advent of the Messiah."

Share: Anti-Semitism (hatred of the Jews) is on the rise globally. Have you witnessed it? How can faithful Christians combat it? Are we preaching a Gospel that is Good News for Jews as much as it is for Gentiles?

_____

_____

_____

_____

Read: We must also *guard against legalism*, which embraces the "old" at the expense of the "new" and limits our expectations of what God wants to and can do today. Near the end of chapter 4, I expand on how contemporary legalism can lead us to focus on the forms: the temple (building), the liturgy, the traditions and the creeds. I also state that falling out of sync with God's timing paralyzes us spiritually because "it causes us to relegate our expectations to something that we believe will happen in the future, when in reality it is already here." And I talk about the consequence of all this—inactive believers who hover around a temple and live innocuously inside a religious system, at best. Or at worst, they become prisoners in a doctrinal POW camp and their main hope is that they will be liberated when their Commander in Chief returns.

Share: Reflect on some contemporary examples of where legalism has caused Christians to focus on the "forms" of our faith rather than on the person in whom we have faith, Jesus Christ.

Deeper: Give an example of where the Church has relegated our expectations to "something that we believe will happen in the future, when in reality it is already here."

_____

_____

Read: Jesus' Ekklesia and the manifestation of the Kingdom of God are two sides of the same coin. We must learn how to share this with others not just in theological terms, but also in tangible demonstrations of God's presence and power that bless and benefit them. In Romans 14:17 Paul declares, "For the kingdom of God is not eating and drinking, but righteousness and peace and joy in the Holy Spirit." Paul declares that the Kingdom of God is about the *living and active presence of Jesus at* *work in us and through us*, touching the people and places *around us* to take "righteousness and peace and joy in the Holy Spirit" to them. In chapter 5, I talk about how this relates to the Ekklesia:

> Unrighteousness, despair and sorrow constitute the lethal social cocktail that the Gates of Hades dispense constantly to individuals and to society. Jesus empowered the Ekklesia to right those wrongs not just in the lives of its members, but also with transforming and catalytic deeds in the marketplace.

To illustrate this important point, you have read in chapter 5 about a dynamic transformation movement in Vallejo, California, and about a company called Michael's Transportation Services, led by Mr. Michael Brown. Here are some ways in which "righteousness and peace and joy in the Holy Spirit" are coming to this city:

- Michael Brown discovered that *there is just as powerful an anointing for ministry in the marketplace as there is for ministry in the pulpit*, and he enthroned Jesus as the CEO of his company.
- "Transformation Vallejo" was born, with the vision of bringing together churches, businesses, schools and government entities to *meet the felt needs of the city*, with prayer evangelism as the biblical model and "street adoption" as the primary implementation strategy.
- The mayor asked those involved in Transformation Vallejo to dedicate the city to God. They did, and today there is clear evidence that transformation has taken root and is fast expanding all over the city.
- Kingdom-focused programs were developed—like the high school Emerging Gentlemen's Program, Campus Transformation Clubs and Michael's Transportation Training Services. These nurture positive character qualities, as well as develop *job skills and training* for vulnerable youth and those who formerly were incarcerated.
- The issue of systemic poverty was addressed when Michael Brown sold 99 percent of his company to his employees, *turning every worker into an owner* and addressing the growing gap between the "haves" and the "have-nots."
- Leaders in Vallejo from every walk of life continue to recognize that *transforming a city involves embracing everything and everyone in it* and claiming the exhortation of 1 Corinthians 4:20, "For the kingdom of God does not consist in words but in power."

Share: How is the leadership team of Transformation Vallejo fostering greater "righteousness and peace and joy" in the city?

_____

_____

_____

Deeper: As part of Jesus' Ekklesia, how are you responding to the felt needs of your city with more than just words, so that the people might experience the power of God at work? If not yet, where might you start?

_____

_____

_____

Read: The Vallejo testimony, and others that you will read about in the coming *Ekklesia* chapters, illustrate that the world needs "good news," not just "good advice." If we believe God's promise to pour out His Spirit on all people, and if we embrace our commission to partner with God to disciple nations, then, as I say in chapter 5, we must "admit that we face pressing theological and structural challenges to live up to that outcome." Something is missing in our proclamation, for example, because people are not responding to it as the Scriptures say they should. I suggest that we lack the deeds to demonstrate and validate the relevance of our message.

We are saved by grace through faith in Jesus, yes, but we must acknowledge that deeds are intrinsically linked to the nature and proclamation of the Kingdom of God throughout Scripture, in addition to being our message's validators. In Matthew 25:35–36, Jesus Himself described the criteria for nations to meet with His approval: feeding the hungry, giving water to the thirsty, providing lodging for the homeless, clothing the naked and caring for and comforting those in prison. Faith without works is dead!

In Matthew 7:21 Jesus says, "Not everyone who says [words] to Me, 'Lord, Lord' will enter the kingdom of heaven, but he who does [deeds] the will of My Father who is in heaven."

James 1:27 states, "Pure and undefiled religion in the sight of our God and Father is this: to visit orphans and widows in their distress, and to keep oneself unstained by the world."

Share: In what ways do we often give our time, our talents and our money . . . without really giving our heart?

_____

_____

_____

Session Summary

- When Jesus came proclaiming the Gospel of the Kingdom, He signaled a radical and irreversible shift in the message to be proclaimed that would become the "new normal."

- The Gospel of the Kingdom can be summarized as simply as this: Jesus is a *present reality*! He is at work in the midst of His Ekklesia to inject the leaven of the Kingdom into the fiber of society, in order to transform not only people, but also institutions, cities and nations.

- The danger of clinging to the Law and the Prophets is that we focus mostly on what God did in the past or promises to do in the future, and as a result, we fall out of step (out of sync) with what God is doing and wants to do in the present.

- The emerging Ekklesia in places like Vallejo, California, is doing the work of God in the public square. Words are being matched with deeds, and whole cities are being transformed.

- Transformation does not happen without personal cost. You cannot change what you don't love first.

Transformed Living

Read: Step 4 of prayer evangelism is to *proclaim* the Good News of Jesus, declaring, "The kingdom of God has come near to you" (Luke 10:9).

Prayer evangelism is progressive. As we have been discovering, when we "bless and speak peace" (step 1), the spiritual climate begins to change. When we offer genuine "fellowship" (step 2), trust is developed, hearts are softened and needs are shared. When we "minister" (step 3) lovingly by first responding to felt needs with prayers of faith combined with action, expecting miracles, the door is opened for the presence of the Lord to meet those needs. What we have traditionally viewed as "preaching the Gospel" now becomes a natural opportunity, prepared by the Holy Spirit, to lead our new friends to Christ.

You have been progressing gradually through these four steps of prayer evangelism from Luke 10, which I listed for you both here and in the book. Prayer evangelism is a lifestyle that Jesus designed to bring about a spiritual climate change wherever it is practiced. One of the desired outcomes of these teachings is that you will experience the power and presence of the Lord Jesus changing you and your spheres of influence. Prayer evangelism is the key to that experience.

Share: What has been your experience so far? What is the farthest you have gotten in the four steps? What was the result? Don't feel pressured or discouraged if you are still on step 1. Keep at it. Jesus is coming to your city, and for this it is essential that, like the seventy He sent out in Luke 10, you prepare the way for Him.

Your **Personal Life Application** this week is to continue steps 1 through 3 of prayer evangelism, but now add step 4, *proclaiming* that "the kingdom of God has come near."

Just as the Holy Spirit opened the door for you to pray and minister to someone's felt needs, this same Spirit is preparing the way for you to share Jesus with your new friend. Don't force it. If the timing is not right for proclamation, patiently continue to implement steps 1 through 3.

Your **Group Life Application** is to identify a social gap that represents a manifestation of the Gates of Hades in your city/region and discern under the guidance of the Holy Spirit how to respond to it. Once again, as listed in Ephesians, these unreconciled social gaps that exist in the earthly realm are ethnic division, religious disunity, ministerial competition, discord between genders, family strife and marketplace injustice (in business, education or government).

Go deeper in your discussion, reflecting on your reading of Ephesians. Where do you see these social gaps in the world today? How do you see them manifesting locally? How is Satan using them to keep people in bondage, "locked up" and fighting with one another? As you share together in your meeting, is the Holy Spirit raising up one of these six areas that you might feel a calling to respond to as an eGroup? If so, list it below.

_____

_____

_____

_____

Eventually, all these gaps must be dealt with, but if the Holy Spirit leads you to focus on a particular one, this could be the point of inception for a move of God in your city. If you are uncertain, pause even now and take it to the Lord in prayer.

Your first step after prayer should be seeking to understand the problem in a deeper way. Whom can you talk to about this issue? The mayor, police chief, counselors, pastors, business leaders or local citizens? Learn from the examples I mentioned in my book's introduction. What questions could you ask to gain deeper understanding?

Take a few minutes to discuss this application as a group. Write down a preliminary action plan on the lines that follow, and accept some assignments either individually or as a group to seek wisdom and direction, gather information and report back at your next session.

_____

_____

_____

_____

_____

Ekklesia Prayer and Ministry

As Session 4 comes to a conclusion, take a few minutes to share prayer requests for yourself and others. Do you have any updates to report from last week's prayers? Are there any testimonies from those who received prayer? Once again as time allows, share in prayer and personal ministry, as the Spirit leads, for anything that has come to the surface during your time together today. Pray specifically for the action steps that you will take together and individually this week. Take notes here so you can remember the prayer requests:

_____

_____

_____

_____

_____

Reading Assignment

In preparation for Session 5, read chapter 6 in *Ekklesia*, "A Fuller Understanding of the Cross."

Daily Devotions

Read: Ephesians 6:17 says "the sword of the Spirit" is "the word of God." Take this to heart as you read, reflect and pray on the Scriptures below. Be encouraged to "stand firm" on the amazing truth and authority of the Word of God. Always pray for the Holy Spirit to illuminate your reading with insight and application for your personal life, family and ministry. Enjoy it!

Day One—Jeremiah 29:10–14

God has a plan and purpose for your life. What promises does His plan include? Is there an experience in your past that feels to you like "banishment and exile"? Ask God for forgiveness and reconciliation. Ask Him to bring you back home and give you hope for the future.

Day Two—Genesis 12:1–9

What is God calling you to leave behind right now to follow Him more closely? What are the blessings He promises? What kind of a legacy would you like to leave for future generations?

Day Three—1 Corinthians 1:18–31

Why does the "word of the cross" often sound like foolishness to the world? To preach the "Gospel of the Kingdom" is to "preach Christ crucified," as verse 23 puts it. Why is this part of our message so foundational, and how do some of the other verses you are looking at this week help explain why?

Day Four—Galatians 5:16–26

What "deeds of the flesh" (verse 19) are keeping you bound to the Law rather than experiencing true freedom in Christ? Which of the "fruits of the Spirit" (see verses 22–23) need cultivating in your life in order for you to have a greater impact in your sphere of influence? What does it mean to you to "walk by the Spirit" (verse 25) as a practical reality in your life?

Day Five—Ephesians 5:21–33

Why is mutual submission out of reverence for Christ so important in a marriage? If you are a wife, reflect deeply on verses 22–24. If you are a husband, reflect deeply on verses 25–30. How does verse 31 speak to the intimacy that God intends for marriage? How does this passage relate to other relationships? To the Church?

Day Six—John 15:1–17

Describe ways in which you are drawing your life from Jesus, like the connection between a vine and its branches. Why does Jesus want you to "bear much fruit" as His disciple (verse 8)? How does keeping the commandments and abiding in Jesus' love (see verse 10) reflect the connection between the "Law and the Prophets" and the "Gospel of the Kingdom of God"? Why is it important to lay down your life, as verse 13 talks about, to reach the world for Jesus?

Day Seven—Your eGroup meets again! Yahoo!

SESSION 5

What this lesson is about:

Jesus' death at the cross reached a stunning climax when He shouted, "It is finished!" But, what exactly was finished? The answer lies in comprehending not only what He did for us, but also what He did to the devil at the cross.

What you will walk away with:

You will come to realize that far from resembling a POW camp cowering behind enemy lines, the Church—even if in a weak condition, as General Wainwright was when he first heard the liberating truth that Japan had been defeated—can and must begin to walk as Jesus' Ekklesia. With an authority that emanates from newly found truths, the Church must walk straight into the enemy's domain and declare, "Our Commander in Chief has defeated your commander in chief." You will come to see the cross as the place of total defeat for the devil and his demons, because it was there that Jesus took away their weapons and made a "public spectacle" of them, parading them as a defeated army. Armed with that illumination, you will be able to stand firm, wearing the full armor of God and expectant that "the God of peace will soon crush Satan under your feet" (Romans 16:20). What an exhilarating and victorious prospect!

Sharing Life

Watch: Play the video introduction for Session 5. This session is based on chapter 6 in *Ekklesia*, "A Fuller Understanding of the Cross."

Pray Together: Dear Lord, we praise You today for Your unconditional love for this world and everyone in it. We thank You for sending Jesus as our Savior and friend. During this session, help us come to an even fuller understanding of the power of the cross to defeat sin and the devil. Fill us with Your Holy Spirit, and set us on the way as Your Ekklesia, to reclaim everything that You have already redeemed. To that end, illuminate the eyes of our spiritual understanding to grasp the fullness of the authority You have entrusted to us over all the power of the evil one. Yes, Lord, help us see the cross for everything it represents and all that emanates from it. In Jesus' name, Amen.

Read: Begin this session by reviewing your **Life Applications** from Session 4.

Share: Your **Personal Life Application** this past week was to continue steps 1 through 3 of prayer evangelism, but also to add step 4, which is to *proclaim*. Were you able to complete this application? Share your experience with the group.

If you are not there yet, be patient and continue to implement steps 1 through 3. Remember 2 Peter 3:9: "The Lord is not slow about His promise, as some count slowness, but is patient toward you, not wishing for any to perish but for all to come to repentance."

Your **Group Life Application** was to identify one of the six social gaps Paul described in his letter to the Ephesians that exist in your city or region and begin to respond to it in a tangible way in order to help close that gap.

Which social gap did your eGroup choose to explore?

_____

What initial steps did you take to speak with people in your community or region, gather information and begin to identify the felt needs related to this issue?

_____

_____

_____

Jot down your findings here and report them to your group:

_____

_____

_____

_____

_____

At the end of this session, you will assess where you are in this process and determine additional steps that you might take with other members of your eGroup, empowered by the Holy Spirit and confident that Jesus' Ekklesia will defeat the Gates of Hades.

Transformed Thinking

Read: Chapter 6 of *Ekklesia* teaches that the Great Commission, like a coin, has two sides. One side is the individual mandate to preach the Gospel to every person. We find this in Mark 16:15, where Jesus says, "Go into all the world and *preach the gospel to all creation*" (emphasis added).

The other side of the Great Commission is the corporate mandate to disciple nations. This is described in Matthew 28:19–20, where Jesus commanded us, "Go therefore and *make disciples of all the nations*, baptizing them in the name of the Father and the Son and the Holy Spirit, teaching them to observe all that I commanded you; and lo, I am with you always, even to the end of the age" (emphasis added).

Both the personal and corporate mandates of the Great Commission tell us to "go" in Jesus' name. Historically speaking, the Church has done a better job of leading people to Christ than it has of making disciples of all the nations. Even in nations where there is a high percentage of born-again believers, it is rare to identify the correlations we should rightfully expect to see in society as a result of that, including safety and security, transparent government, a productive economy, access to medical care and educational opportunities for all.

Remember, for a nation to be discipled, what happens in the pulpit and in the congregation on Sunday must impact the marketplace every day of the week with "righteousness and peace and joy in the Holy Spirit" (Romans 14:17). Why do we see a disconnect between what is preached inside the four walls of the Church and how it plays out in the marketplace? In the book, I suggest that it is because the Church has not been as intentional about discipling the nations as it has been about discipling individuals. We must integrate these two dimensions of the Great Commission, and how to do that is the central theme of my book, as well as this study.

Share: Why has it been easier for the Church to focus on preaching to individuals, often to the neglect of the needs of society?

_____

_____

Deeper: At this point in our *Ekklesia* study, what is hardest for you to grasp about the concept of discipling a nation?

_____

_____

Read: To transform nations, the Church today must realize, embrace and practice the principle that Jesus came to seek and save not just the lost, but "*that which was lost*," meaning everything that was lost when Adam and Eve sinned, including the marketplace—the combination of business, education and government—which is the heart of a nation. We find this important distinction on clear display at the conclusion of Jesus' encounter with the despised tax collector Zaccheus. Much to the amazement of the crowd, Jesus said, "Today salvation has come to *this house*, because he, too, is a son of Abraham. For the Son of Man has come *to seek and to save that which was lost*" (Luke 19:9–10, emphasis added).

Jesus explained this fascinating and surprising outcome—that a greedy person like Zaccheus had decided to give half his wealth to the poor and offer to make restitution to everyone he had wronged—by pointing out that salvation had come to Zaccheus's "house" or "household," which in New Testament times included family, business, employees, servants and possessions. In other words, all of *"that which was lost"* had now been saved.

Share: What is something that you would like to see saved in your "household"? In your city?

Read: To understand the greater dimension of what Jesus redeemed and reconciled, and has now sent us to reclaim as His Ekklesia, we need to revisit what happened in the Garden of Eden and ask what was lost. In the book, I summarized the answer this way:

1. The eternal destiny of every human being was lost because sin raised a wall of separation between God and man.

2. The relationship between man and woman was lost since Adam and Eve's relationship ceased to be harmonious.

3. The marketplace was lost, which the Garden of Eden represented. (This is our key point under discussion.)

We accept the biblical truth that Jesus died to redeem people, but we also need to ask a different, albeit complementary, question: Did Jesus die for something more than people's souls? Think about that in light of these two passages of Scripture, which you can read aloud as a group:

> For it was the Father's good pleasure for all the fullness to dwell in Him [Jesus], and through Him to reconcile *all things* to Himself, having made peace through the blood of His cross; through Him, I say, whether *things on earth* or *things in heaven*.
>
> Colossians 1:19–20, emphasis added

In Him we have redemption through His blood, the forgiveness of our trespasses, according to the riches of His grace . . . the summing up of *all things* in Christ, *things in the heavens* and *things on the earth*.

Ephesians 1:7, 10, emphasis added

Share: How many "things" are to be reconciled? Where?

_____

_____

Deeper: How central is this to our understanding of what took place on the cross?

_____

_____

Read: These passages refer to the "fullness of the Atonement." In *Ekklesia*, you read that Jesus paid the price to redeem both individuals and nations. Because of the cross, not only have you received the forgiveness of your sins and the promise of eternal life, but your relationship with your heavenly Father has been restored. He sees you now as a son or daughter fully redeemed. And the same is true for everything else that was lost in addition to people. The cross provided redemption for the marketplace, as well. *This truth provides us with biblical grounds for the Ekklesia, operating 24/7 all over the city, to reclaim the marketplace.* To that effect, God has called you to be His representative to the world.

In my imaginary exchange between God and the devil that you read near the end of chapter 6, I described the "fight of the ages" that took place at the cross. In that moment God added a new rule—*grace*—that totally disarmed the devil and any claims he thought he could make on either the people or the things that were lost. The final result was, "Sorry, devil. Game over!"

As Colossians 2:15 declares, "When He [Jesus] had disarmed the rulers and authorities, He made a public display of them, having triumphed over them through Him." And as I say at the end of the chapter,

> The blood shed by our Lord paid the price not only to redeem our souls, but also to redeem everything that was lost: people, business, education and government. And there is nothing the devil can do to reverse it.
>
> When Jesus cried, "It is finished!" it was not an agonizing gasp, but a triumphant shout proclaiming victory . . .

Share: How does it make you feel to know that you have been redeemed and now God sees you as a son or daughter?

_____

_____

How does it impact you to know that the atonement of Jesus also paid the price for *everything* that was lost, so that what has been redeemed can now be reclaimed for God's Kingdom?

_____

_____

Deeper: Because Jesus won the "fight of the ages" on the cross, what victories can we expect to win today personally and in the marketplace?

_____

_____

Read: In the book, I gave you a compelling example from history of General William Wainwright, the only American general taken prisoner by the Japanese during World War II. He remained a POW after the war had ended. Why? Because the truth that Japan had surrendered was kept from him. When the news finally came, General Wainwright walked straight into the Japanese commandant's office and declared: "My commander in chief has defeated your commander in chief; I am in charge here now!" It was the truth that set him free and empowered him to exercise authority over all the power of the enemy.

This same truth is needed today, in order for the Ekklesia to be set free to fulfill the Great Commission, including the discipling of nations. There is no place for the contemporary Church to resemble a POW camp behind enemy lines. It must reclaim as its inheritance "the very ends of the earth" (Psalm 2:8).

Share: How are people in the Church and in our world held captive and in bondage today?

_____

_____

Deeper: If you believe that the truth about Jesus sets people free, what does it imply for your mission and ministry as a member of the Ekklesia?

_____

_____

Session Summary

- The Great Commission, as recorded in Mark 16:15 and Matthew 28:19–20, has two sides: to preach to individuals and to disciple nations.
- Jesus came "to seek and to save" every part of creation, including the marketplace—business, education and government.
- Whole "households" like Zaccheus's are meant to come to the Lord and experience His blessings.
- When Jesus won the "fight of the ages" on the cross, He earned the authority that He now entrusts to His Ekklesia to reclaim everything that was lost.
- Our Commander in Chief is in charge. The truth of what He did for us, and what He did to the devil and his demons at the cross, will set us free.

Transformed Living

Read: Your **Personal Life Application** this week is to *continue to develop a lifestyle of prayer evangelism*. To assist you further as you *bless*, *fellowship*, *minister* and *proclaim*, I encourage you to memorize three passages of Scripture that I quote often. (Use whatever Bible translation is your favorite.) These three Scriptures are foundational to every member of Jesus' Ekklesia:

The Great Promise in John 3:16–17: "For God so loved the world, that He gave His only begotten Son, that whoever believes in Him shall not perish, but have eternal life. For God did not send the Son into the world to judge the world, but that the world might be saved through Him."

The Great Commandment in Matthew 22:37–39: "And He said to him, 'You shall love the Lord your God with all your heart, and with all your soul, and with all your mind.' This is the great and foremost commandment. The second is like it, 'You shall love your neighbor as yourself.'"

The Great Commission in Matthew 28:18–20: "And Jesus came up and spoke to them, saying, 'All authority has been given to Me in heaven and on earth. Go therefore and make disciples of all the nations, baptizing them in the name of the Father and the Son and the Holy Spirit, teaching them to observe all that I commanded you; and lo, I am with you always, even to the end of the age.'"

Some people struggle with memorizing Scripture. If you are one of them, the first thing to do is to claim victory and ask the Holy Spirit to help you, because Jesus said that the Holy Spirit will "guide you into all the truth"

(John 16:13). Declare, "I *can* memorize Scripture because I desire God's words of life and truth to reside in me."

Also, begin with prayer. Next, read the individual passage several times. Under the guidance of the Holy Spirit, let its full meaning sink in. Now break it down phrase by phrase and repeat it until you have memorized the whole passage. Then—and here is an important key—share it with someone else right away. With God's help, you can do it! As your eGroup meets next week, you can pair up and practice with one another.

Your **Group Life Application** is to take a next step in responding to the specific social gap that you have identified in your city or region. Specifically, the goal is to match words with deeds, so that the Gates of Hades will come down. Be expecting God to do miracles in the process, as was the case in Vallejo with Michael Brown and his associates.

In light of the information you gathered last week and the felt needs you began to identify, what is God putting on your heart as a "next step" to respond to those needs in a tangible way? Don't leave out the fact that divine intervention is required all along the way, but specifically in step 3 of prayer evangelism, *minister*. Discuss some ideas now and jot them down. Then take a few moments to pray about them.

_____

_____

_____

_____

_____

Is the Holy Spirit bringing clarity? If so, begin developing your action plan right now. How can you *minister* into the specific situation that you have chosen so that the *proclamation* of the Gospel of the Kingdom—that Jesus is a present reality whose love and power are available to meet needs both in people and in your community—is matched with good deeds that validate your words, including miracles? Remember this important insight from this session's chapter of *Ekklesia*:

> We must admit that we face pressing theological and structural challenges to live up to that outcome [of seeing nations saved]. One of those challenges we face has to do with proclamation. Something is missing, because people are not responding to our proclamation as the Scriptures tell us they should. I submit to you that we lack the deeds that would demonstrate and validate the relevance of the words in the message we preach.

If you don't have clarity yet about how to add deeds to your words, you may need to do some more fact finding. Talk to some key people in your community, or spend some more time in discussion and prayer. The latter is key, because God is the Lord of the harvest and He is the one sending you into the fields to do the gathering.

What will your next steps be? Give assignments, either to individuals or teams in your eGroup, and keep the ball rolling!

_____

_____

_____

_____

_____

This is a process. Every eGroup needs to hear from God and find its own way forward. The key is to keep moving, expecting that what we usually see taking place within the four walls of the Church will also begin to happen in the public square—changed lives and miracles of salvation, restoration, healing and so much more. Remember that as the Ekklesia, you are a "massive people movement" and a "transforming organism" in operation 24/7 all over town. Rather than being an item on someone else's agenda, the Ekklesia is the agenda setter, and you are part of it. Go for it, in Jesus' name!

Ekklesia Prayer and Ministry

As Session 5 comes to a conclusion, take a few minutes to share prayer requests for yourself and others. Remember to share updates, testimonies and answers to prayer. Once again, as time allows, share in prayer and personal ministry as the Holy Spirit leads. Include prayers of faith for whole "households" to be saved, like the ones we see reported in the New Testament. Take notes here about the prayer needs you have or those you hear about from your group:

_____

_____

_____

_____

_____

Reading Assignment

In preparation for Session 6, read chapters 7 and 8 in *Ekklesia*, "A Fuller Understanding of the Great Commission" and "A Fuller Understanding of Cooperation with God."

Daily Devotions

Read: Here again are some passages of Scripture for each day of the coming week, starting with Day One tomorrow. There are also some questions to spur on your reflections. These sections of Scripture build on the key points we have covered in this session. May God bless you abundantly as you seek a deeper walk with Jesus and a more effective ministry in your sphere of influence.

Day One—Romans 8:12–17

Reflect on these wonderful words that describe our adoption as sons and daughters of a heavenly Father. What are some blessings that you have already received as a child of God? What are some blessings that will one day belong to you for all eternity?

Day Two—John 1:1–14

Who is "*the Word*" that the first and last verses of this passage refer to? What are the qualities that describe Him? Why do some people fail to recognize Jesus for who He really is (see verses 10–11)? What promise is made in verse 12 to those who believe and receive? How have you personally experienced Jesus' grace and truth mentioned in verse 14?

Day Three—Psalm 2:1–12

How do you observe nations conspiring and people plotting in vain today? The Lord says, "Ask of Me, and I will surely give the nations as Your inheritance, and the very ends of the earth as Your possession" (verse 8). Have you asked God for your nation? What will it mean for you personally if you do so? Where will you start?

Day Four—Matthew 25:31–46

According to verse 32, who will be gathered before the Son of Man when He comes in all His glory? Allow this text to speak to you from the perspective of nations, not just individuals. How does this change your reflection on this passage's example of "the sheep and the goats"? Could there be accountability for nations, as well as individuals, when Jesus returns?

Day Five—1 Timothy 2:1–6

Who among "all men" do you find it hardest to pray for? What does verse 4 say God's great desire is? According to verse 6, how did Jesus mediate the deep divide between God and humankind? How might today's passage help you pray differently for those serving in the marketplace?

Day Six—1 John 4:1–6

Reflect further on the story of General Wainwright. I commented in chapter 6 that "because the general did not know the truth—that Japan had been defeated—he continued to behave like a POW. Every order from his captors lacked legitimacy, but not knowing that, he obeyed them." What orders are you unknowingly taking from the enemy? Upon learning the truth, General Wainwright confidently told his captor, "My commander in chief has defeated your commander in chief; I am in charge here now!" How do his words relate to 1 John 4:4, "Greater is He who is in you than he who is in the world"?

Day Seven—your eGroup meets today! Be blessed!

SESSION 6

"Without God we can't, but without us He won't." That maxim has inspired and energized the great missionary thrusts of the last two centuries. It is why in Matthew 28:19–20, Jesus did not issue a Great Commission, but rather a Great Partnership, because He assured us that He would walk alongside us all the way to the end, and in so doing He turned a monumental task into a transformational lifestyle.

You will clearly see how the tipping point in the journey to discipling nations is just like the one at a wedding ceremony, when the couple says, "I do." Everything else flows out of that. You will be inspired by the stories of ordinary people who are today doing extraordinary deeds that began with sincerely uttering the two most powerful words in the English language: "Yes, Lord!" And you will go on to be used by God in ways beyond anything you may have thought or imagined so far. That is the beauty and power of rediscovering your role in Jesus' Ekklesia.

Sharing Life

Watch: Play the video introduction for Session 6. This session is based on chapters 7 and 8 in *Ekklesia*, "A Fuller Understanding of the Great Commission" and "A Fuller Understanding of Cooperation with God."

Pray Together: Dear God, Your Word is awesome! Help us recognize it as the truth and authority from which flows Your power to transform every area of our lives. Today, as we further consider Jesus' commission to disciple nations, please open our eyes to see our nation as something precious in Your sight. With all of its problems and challenges, You have not given up on it, or on the people, places and institutions that make it up. Help us not to give up either. We lift our nation in prayer and ask You to bless it today, while You teach us how to disciple it. And we pray that we ourselves will be transformed first, so that Your power and Your presence will flow from us to our families and our spheres of influence, and from there to our cities and nations. In Jesus' name, Amen.

Read: Begin this session by reviewing your **Life Applications** from Session 5 as a group.

Share: Your **Personal Life Application** this past week was to memorize three key passages of Scripture that are foundational to our mission as Jesus' Ekklesia: John 3:16–17, Matthew 22:37–39 and Matthew 28:18–20. Pair up with someone in your group and take turns reciting these memory verses one by one. Start by sharing which Bible translation you used. If you are not quite there yet with memorizing these passages, keep working at it. Help and encourage one another. (Turn back to "Transformed Living" in Session 5 if you need to review the verses.) The more often you review these passages during the week—in your car, out for a walk, before you fall asleep—the deeper they will go into your heart and soul.

The psalmist declares, "Your word is a lamp to my feet and a light to my path" (Psalm 119:105). How did God light your path with the Scriptures you were memorizing this week?

_____

_____

You were also encouraged to continue developing a lifestyle of prayer evangelism. Whom did you engage with this past week? What opportunities did you have to take relationships deeper and wider? How are you seeing God at work in your life and in the lives of others?

_____

_____

_____

_____

Your **Group Life Application** was to take further action steps together regarding the social gap that has been the focus of your eGroup outreach to the community. What additional steps have you taken, or what steps are still in the planning stages? Discuss your progress together.

_____

_____

Transformed Thinking

Read: Following His resurrection and just prior to His ascension into heaven, Jesus shared some powerful and affirming words with His disciples. Today, we call those words the Great Commission. Let's look once more at the full text recorded in Matthew 28:16–20 (emphasis added):

> But the eleven disciples proceeded to Galilee, to the mountain which Jesus had designated. When they saw Him, they worshiped Him; but some were doubtful. And Jesus came up and spoke to them, saying, "All authority has been given to Me in heaven and on earth. Go therefore and *make disciples of all the nations*, baptizing them in the name of the Father and the Son and the Holy Spirit, teaching them to observe all that I commanded you; and lo, I am with you always, even to the end of the age."

Chapter 7 in *Ekklesia* explains that with these words, *Jesus introduced a radical new lifestyle.* These marching orders caused His followers not only to recognize their call to proclaim the Gospel to individuals, but also to "disciple nations." Jesus' band of disciples were all younger than 33 years old, with little education, no experience traveling outside their home territory and no formal training in preaching to crowds of people. How did this band "turn the world upside down" (see Acts 17:6) in just a matter of years?

Scripture tells us that some among this young band were even doubtful. Yet we can observe throughout the New Testament that they and thousands like them gained strength from the following things as they grew:

- The amazing facts of Jesus' death and resurrection, upon which they were willing to stake their lives.
- The personal example of Jesus' life and ministry, to which they had been eyewitnesses for three years.
- The extraordinary miracles they had been privileged to see up close and personal while Jesus was with them, which God was now performing through their hands, following the outpouring of the Holy Spirit (see Acts 5:12–16; 19:11).
- The assurance Jesus gave them that they would emulate Him: "He who believes in Me, the works that I do, he will do also; and greater works than these he will do" (John 14:12).

These disciples also overcame their doubts specifically as a result of Jesus' affirming words in the Great Commission:

- *"Go!"* Jesus also imparted to them His spiritual authority that came along with His mandate for them to go.
- *"I am with you always."* Jesus promised to be with His followers, even to the end of the age.

Jesus began His charge to disciple nations with the words "All authority has been given to Me in heaven and on earth." Like a runner in a relay race, Jesus was passing the baton to His disciples, promising that His authority, the authority of heaven and earth, would now be accessible to them. And at the very moment when He was about to ascend into heaven, when feelings of fear and abandonment could have easily set in on His followers, Jesus was conveying to them, "Don't worry. I'm departing from you physically, but I will be with you by My Spirit every step of the way."

Jesus' precise promise was, "I am with you always, even to the end of the age." That is why I said in *Ekklesia* that the Great Partnership is an even better term than the Great Commission. He provided us with everything necessary to disciple nations—all authority in heaven and on earth—and His presence alongside us until the task has been accomplished.

Share: How are these two "bookend promises" contained in the Great Commission (Jesus' authority and His presence) designed to give you courage to "go" in His name and disciple nations?

_____

_____

Read: Let's examine *how* the assignment to disciple nations gets fleshed out in greater detail in the book of Acts. Jesus' vision of the Ekklesia was both *inclusive*, in that it welcomed all people, and *expansive*, in that it was intended to reach the whole world: "But you will receive power when the Holy Spirit has come upon you; and you shall be My witnesses both in Jerusalem, and in all Judea and Samaria, and even to the remotest part of the earth" (Acts 1:8). I put it this way in chapter 7: "He told them to begin in the city where they resided (Jerusalem), and next move on to a province (Judea), and then to a nation (Samaria), and after reaching that milestone, to keep on going until they had reached the ends of the earth."

Share: Take a minute to personalize this assignment from Jesus by filling in the blanks:

But you, _____ [insert your name], will receive power when the Holy Spirit has come upon you; and you will be My witnesses in _____ [your city], and in _____ [your state/province], and in _____ [your nation], and even to the remotest part of the earth _____ [a faraway nation].

After everyone in your group has prepared his or her personalized version of Acts 1:8, read your verses aloud together all at the same time. Don't read the bracketed instructions like [insert your name] and [your city]; just include your filled-in blanks. Ready? Set? Go! This gives you a little taste of the spirit of the Great Commission and the Day of Pentecost (when they were all speaking in other tongues) combined.

Read: In chapter 7, I make what I believe is a scholarly and compelling case that the Greek text, from which modern-day translations of the Bible are derived, is unambiguous regarding Jesus' mandate to make disciples *of all the nations*. The proper translation of the Greek makes it clear that Jesus' followers are to make disciples "of" the nations, not just make disciples "in" the nations. We should not be surprised by this emphasis on nations and not just individuals. The Bible mentions the words *nation* and *nations* 589 times! Take turns reading aloud this sampling of Bible references related to the nations (emphasis added throughout):

> I will make you exceedingly fruitful, and I will make *nations* of you, and kings will come forth from you.
>
> Genesis 17:6

> In your seed all the *nations* of the earth shall be blessed, because you have obeyed My voice.
>
> Genesis 22:18

> God also said to him, "I am God Almighty: be fruitful and multiply; a *nation* and a company of *nations* shall come from you, and kings shall come forth from you."
>
> Genesis 35:11

> Ask of Me, and I will surely give the *nations* as Your inheritance, and the very ends of the earth as Your possession.
>
> Psalm 2:8

> This gospel of the kingdom shall be preached in the whole world as a testimony to all the *nations*, and then the end will come.
>
> Matthew 24:14

> All the *nations* will be gathered before Him; and He will separate them from one another, as the shepherd separates the sheep from the goats.
>
> Matthew 25:32

> Go therefore and make disciples of all the *nations*, baptizing them in the name of the Father and the Son and the Holy Spirit.
>
> Matthew 28:19

> But you are a chosen race, a royal priesthood, a holy *nation*, a people for God's own possession, so that you may proclaim the excellencies of Him who has called you out of darkness into His marvelous light.
>
> 1 Peter 2:9

The *nations* will walk by its light, and the kings of the earth will bring their glory into it.

Revelation 21:24

As you reflect on these, remember what I said in chapter 7—that just as God chose the nation of Israel in the Old Testament to be a blessing to the nations of the earth, He also designated a New Testament equivalent to do the same, and that entity is the Ekklesia.

Discuss: Describe some of the parts that make up a nation (business, education, government, etc.). Write them down here, and then pause for prayer, asking God to bless these parts of your nation.

_____

_____

_____

Deeper: If the Church today were to acknowledge that Jesus gave His life for *all* the parts of our nations, how might it change our priorities?

_____

_____

Read: When Jesus says "go," He literally means "as you go on your way," wherever you are and whatever you are doing in life. In chapter 7 I expand on this:

> This meaning reinforces the point that every believer is a minister and that labor is worship, and it defines the Great Commission as a lifestyle, not an occasional task or a special assignment. By the way Christians live—both at home and at work (see Colossians 3:23)—they are to bring transformation to every person, as well as to every sphere of the life of nations they encounter "on their way."

In chapter 8, I present three remarkable testimonies that bear witness to the power and the fruits of this "transformational lifestyle." They involved Ricardo "King" Flores, a pulpit and marketplace minister in Parañaque, Philippines; Francis Oda, an architect from Honolulu, Hawaii, who is currently working on a huge project in the country of Tahiti; and Poncho Murguía, a pulpit and marketplace minister in Ciudad Juárez, Mexico. All three of these men illustrate the importance of the axiom "Without God we can't, but without us He won't."

In Parañaque, what started in a large motel chain that had been used daily by thousands of prostitutes and their clients went on to become an embassy of heaven on earth—an Ekklesia—after the owner hired thirty pastors to "shepherd" the hotel staff according to the principles of prayer evangelism. Thousands came to the Lord, and Exhibit A for the Gates of Hades became a hallmark of God's will on earth. Remember from your reading in the book how that light soon spread to other parts of society? With the heart of an ambassador, King Flores purposefully bridged the gap between the pulpit and the marketplace, and as a result the Philippine Supreme Court, army and national police all underwent transformation training. Corruption was renounced, and the city's seal now reads, "Para-ñaque City—Dedicated to God." What an example of discipling a nation!

Share: Let the Holy Spirit speak to you. As happened in Parañaque, where would you like to see a tangible expression of the Ekklesia established in your city? Can you begin to believe God for it?

_____

_____

Read: Dr. Francis Oda is chairman of the renowned architectural firm Group 70 International. Remember how the president of French Polynesia was so impressed with some of Francis's designs that he asked how Francis had come up with such extraordinary ideas in such a short period of time? And Francis simply stated, "It was God." He also led the president and his family to the Lord and baptized them. The story continues to this day—as of the time of this writing, Group 70 International had been awarded another multibillion-dollar project in Tahiti.

Share: Reflect on an area in your life right now where you need creative insights and solutions from God . . . perhaps in your home, church, work-place, marriage or family. Have you asked God to provide these insights and solutions, as He did for Francis? Take a couple of minutes of silence in your eGroup for personal reflection and prayer on this. Start by saying yes to God in your hearts and asking Him for the guidance and power you need. Then take time to both write down and share with your group how God is speaking to you.

_____

_____

Read: In chapter 8 I also told you the story of Pastor Poncho Murguía in Ciudad Juárez, Mexico, a city *formerly* known as the "murder capital of the world." Praying and fasting for his city, Poncho caught the attention of a local journalist and eventually the mayor. Sensing the Spirit at work, the mayor called upon Poncho to help him clean up the notorious El CERESO Prison, which was controlled by the drug cartels. If anywhere on earth could embody the Gates of Hades on earth, it was that prison! Yet under the direction of Pastor Poncho, and with the support of the army and police, El CERESO was reclaimed from the cartels without a single shot being fired. The Ekklesia within it then exploded with growth.

The streets of the city were still filled with violence, however. They were like a war zone. The turning point came when Poncho and a fellow Ekklesia pastor went to a high place to adopt the city and declared over it, "Juárez, you are no longer an orphan city. You have been adopted by your Father in heaven, and by us." Today, Ciudad Juárez is one of the safest cities in Mexico. Under Pastor Poncho Murguía's ongoing leadership, and with an army of partners who have also said yes to God, transformation continues to spread across the city and nation. Biblical paradigms and principles, empowered by the Holy Spirit, have begun to touch every aspect of society.

Share: Why is it important that when everyone else is running away from a problem, the Ekklesia runs toward it? (Hint: According to the book and earlier sessions, what keys have we been given to defeat the Gates of Hades?)

Read: These testimonies from King Flores, Francis Oda and Poncho Murguía are indeed extraordinary . . . but as members of the Ekklesia, we are all invited to say yes to God. When we do, He promises to use us right where we are planted and turn the ordinary into the extraordinary. What holds us back from partnering with God? Here are the two barriers I suggest in chapter 8:

> I submit that the reason we are reluctant to see ourselves as partners with God is due to one of two factors. The first one is excessive humility, and the second is an ignorance of how special we are in God's eyes, or undervaluing ourselves. . . .
>
> Those whom God uses are genuinely humble people, because He "resists the proud, but gives grace to the humble" (James 4:6 NKJV). The devil knows that those who are humble will not easily succumb to pride, so he tempts them with *excessive* humility. Pride overshoots, and excessive humility undershoots. Both miss the mark and end up preventing people from being used by God for extraordinary exploits.

In Ephesians 2:8–10, the apostle Paul makes perfectly clear the important relationship between faith and works:

> For by grace you have been saved through faith; and that not of yourselves, it is the gift of God; not as a result of works, so that no one may boast. For we are His workmanship, created in Christ Jesus for good works, which God prepared beforehand so that we would walk in them.

We are saved by grace, yes, but then we are called to good works. And every great journey in life begins with a first step. The devil can no longer accuse us before God's throne, because he has been defeated. Revelation 12:11 declares, "And they overcame him because of the blood of the Lamb and because of the word of their testimony, and they did not love their life even when faced with death."

Share: For reasons that defy comprehension this side of eternity, God chooses and waits for our cooperation to do some things. If you were being really vulnerable, which factor would you say is most likely to hold you back from saying yes to God and answering His call—excessive pride ("I can do it myself") or excessive humility ("I'm not good enough")?

Session Summary

- The Great Commission has a dual mandate to disciple people and nations.
- Jesus made provision for us to overcome our doubts by assuring us of His authority and presence through the Holy Spirit.
- When Jesus says "go," He literally means "as you go on your way."
- Setbacks become setups when we minister in the marketplace, responding to the needs of others in the power of the Holy Spirit.
- "Without God we can't, but without us He won't." We are all called to partner with God by moving from *contemplation* to *cooperation*.
- It all starts when we say "Yes, Lord!" Those are perhaps the two most important words in any language.

Transformed Living

Read: Your **Personal Life Application** this week is to *Adopt Your Street* in prayer. You can register your street adoption at http://adopt.transform ourworld.org/en/adopt. (Note that in Adoption step 2, after naming the street you wish to adopt, you can check the box "Show Nearby Adoptions" below the map to see the locations of other street adoptions near your location.) Adopting your street also provides tremendous encouragement to others who are also rediscovering Jesus' Ekklesia.

Street adoption is an important way to practice a lifestyle of prayer evangelism and respond to the dual mandate of the Great Commission. Follow the four-step strategy Jesus taught His disciples in Luke 10: *bless, fellowship, minister* and *proclaim*. Your street adoption can focus on the homes and neighbors on the street where you live, or it can focus on your office building or construction site and your co-workers, or the school you attend and your classmates, or your local City Hall and government officials . . .

Join the movement! There is no limit to where God wants to use you. Start by asking the Holy Spirit to speak to you about where you should focus your street adoption. Ask the Holy Spirit to give you a burden for a "piece of turf" and the people and places represented there, so that your prayers can lead to tangible deeds done in Jesus' name. Pastor Greg Pagh testifies this about his street adoption experience:

> I have been blessed to lead a street adoption prayer movement in my home state of Minnesota in the United States. We call it *Bless Minnesota—Adopt Your Street* (www.BlessMN.org). Hundreds of believers are putting "legs to their prayers" and becoming a blessing to others. We were inspired by the testimony that originally came out of Newark, New Jersey, and today people are adopting streets in prayer in dozens of countries all over the world.

Your **Group Life Application** is similar in nature. As you have seen from reading *Ekklesia*, to defeat the Gates of Hades we must do battle in both the "heavenly places" and the "unreconciled social gaps" where evil is entrenched. By proclaiming a spirit of adoption over your city, as Poncho Murguía did in Ciudad Juárez, Mexico, you are putting the enemy on notice and declaring, "The Ekklesia is in town! We're here to stay, and we will win the victory!"

You are also claiming Jesus' promises from the Great Commission of His authority and presence. You are declaring in the heavens what you expect to see happen on earth. This is exactly what began to happen when the Ekklesia in Mexico, under Poncho's leadership, decided to adopt sicarios, or hit men, in prayer. Soon afterward, the Gates of Hades lost some of its key players to the Ekklesia.

Invite the counsel of your eGroup leader as you talk and pray about identifying a high place in your city or region where you can go as a group. Once you get there, make a declaration over your city that reflects a spirit of adoption on your part:

> _____ [insert your city], you are no longer an orphan. You have already been adopted by your heavenly Father, and today, we adopt you.

And always keep in mind that prayer is not the end, but the means for God to intervene in the lives of those you are praying for, usually in the form of a miracle so that they will come to salvation. Here is Dr. Pagh's description of that event involving Bless Minnesota:

> On May 5, 2016, Bless Minnesota pulpit and marketplace leaders, led by my wife, Colleen, and I, made a declaration from the top of the tallest building in the State of Minnesota, the IDS Tower in Minneapolis. Simultaneously, "street adopters" all over the state were also making this declaration from high places in their cities. Since we declared a spirit of adoption over Minnesota, an increase in love, compassion, unity and spiritual authority to bind and loose in Jesus' name has become evident.

Ekklesia Prayer and Ministry

Take a few moments once again to share testimonies of answered prayer, ongoing needs and new prayer requests. As time allows, close with a period of Spirit-led prayer and ministry to one another. Pray that God will increase your passion for reaching the lost in your city or region and that every member of your eGroup will be led to adopt a street in prayer this week.

You can take some notes here to help you continue to pray for one another throughout the week:

_____

_____

_____

_____

_____

Reading Assignment

In preparation for Session 7, read chapter 9 in *Ekklesia*, "A Fuller Understanding of New Testament Baptisms."

Daily Devotions

Read: Most of us are not wired for a lot of quiet time. We like to be around people and be engaged in conversation and activity. The Lord has had to teach many of us the importance of time alone to pray, think, read and draw closer to Him. In this journey, Jesus' personal example should encourage us. He drew strength from His time alone with His Father in order to serve others with passion all the way to the cross.

Day One—Matthew 13:1–23

How do the four kinds of soil and ground conditions in the parable of the sower represent the various ways that people can either accept or reject God's Word? Reflect on the soil conditions right now in your personal life. How about that of your local church? Where do some weeds need to be pulled out or some soil cultivated? Where have you been given opportunities to scatter good seed?

Day Two—2 Corinthians 12:1–10

What impact do you sense that Paul's visions and revelations had on his life when he was "caught up into Paradise and heard inexpressible words, which a man is not permitted to speak" (verse 4)? Even in the face of suffering with what Paul describes as a "thorn in the flesh," God spoke uplifting words that came as a great comfort. What were those words? Has your experience of grace been so sufficient that you, too, could say, "When I am weak, then I am strong" (verse 10)?

Day Three—Isaiah 55:6–12

As you read this passage, recognize that God invites you to seek Him and call upon Him. What a privilege! Imagine the "thoughts" and "ways" of the Lord (see verse 8). As we consider the mission of the Ekklesia to disciple nations, how reassuring it is to hear God say, "So will My word be which goes forth from My mouth; it will not return to Me empty, without accomplishing what I desire, and without succeeding in the matter for which I sent it" (verse 11). For this reason we can "go out with joy and be led forth with peace" (verse 12).

Day Four—Matthew 6:25–34

When you worry about your life, what are the two or three things that are at the top of your list? What is the antidote to worry? What are some of the "all these things" described in verse 33 that God promises to add for those who choose to seek *first* His Kingdom and His righteousness?

Day Five—2 Chronicles 7:11–22

What are the conditions the Lord placed on Solomon for retaining His blessing? Is it possible that God's love for us is unconditional, but that His blessing and protection are conditioned by our willingness to pray, seek His face and follow His ways? What does God want to teach you from this passage today?

Day Six—John 14:1–7

How have you found belief, trust and faith in God to be the antidote for a troubled heart? Aside from what heaven may look like, what promises about heaven does Jesus make in these verses? How do you feel about the statement in verse 6 in which He makes these claims: "I am the way, and the truth, and the life; no one comes to the Father but through Me"? Will you stake your life on this statement? Will you share this truth with others?

Day Seven—your eGroup meets today! Have a wonderful gathering!

SESSION 7

Skewed assumptions related to water baptism and to the baptism in the Holy Spirit have created major walls of division and impeded the Ekklesia from embracing her full mission. A closer look at three different kinds of baptisms in the New Testament will point the way to "a more excellent biblical way."

What you will walk away with:

You will tap into a closer relationship with the Holy Spirit that will give you power, so that like the apostle Paul, your "preaching" will be a "demonstration of the Spirit and of power" (1 Corinthians 2:4). You will also come to understand in a deeper way the baptism of the Holy Spirit and its relationship to water baptism. Furthermore, you will gain insight into why so many sincere believers lack the spiritual power to enjoy a victorious life, both at a personal level and in the marketplace.

Sharing Life

Watch: Play the video introduction for Session 7. This session is based on chapter 9 in *Ekklesia*, "A Fuller Understanding of New Testament Baptisms."

Pray Together: Dear Lord, thank You for the gift of these friends in our group, and for the opportunity to grow deeper in faith as we study and learn from Your Word together. Remind us that transformation is a journey and that even though we are called to "disciple nations," baptizing and teaching them in Your name, it all starts right where we are—in our homes, schools, places of work and communities. Please continue to baptize us with Your Holy Spirit so that we will never run dry! In Jesus' name, Amen.

Read: Begin this session by reviewing your **Life Applications** from Session 6.

Share: Your **Personal Life Application** this past week was to *Adopt Your Street* in prayer. You were asked to register your street adoption at http://

adopt.transformourworld.org/en/adopt. Adopting your street is a most practical way to jump-start your lifestyle of prayer evangelism, and as you can now see, it gets you involved in the dual mandate of the Great Commission.

Share with your group which street you adopted and what the Lord has put on your heart about the people and places there. This is an ongoing **Life Application** because prayer evangelism, as implemented through your street adoption, is a lifestyle, not a program. As you continue to pray and minister, the Lord might use your street adoption as a "point of inception" for transformation in your city (a concept I talk about more in chapter 15 of *Ekklesia*). Imagine the impact of one hundred, one thousand or ten thousand such adoptions!

Your **Group Life Application** was similar in nature. I encouraged you to seek the Lord for His wisdom and timing regarding a group declaration of a spirit of adoption over your city or region, and I challenged you to go to a high place as a group and make this declaration together:

_____ [insert your city], you are no longer an orphan. You have already been adopted by your heavenly Father, and today, we adopt you.

Where are you in this process? Have you taken this step to declare a spirit of adoption over your city or region? By doing so, you commit to loving the people and places there in the same way that parents promise to love and care for an adopted child. Remember, we cannot transform what we don't love first. Jot down any details here related to your decision as an eGroup to take this step together. Once you make this declaration, it is important to continue to walk in the authority you have been given.

_____

_____

_____

_____

Transformed Thinking

Read: In the Great Commission, Jesus not only tells His disciples to go and make disciples of all nations, but He also instructs them to *baptize nations*. Most of us are familiar with the baptism of individuals, but how do you baptize a nation? As I teach in chapter 9, before this question can be answered, we must gain a fuller understanding of New Testament baptisms. The New Testament mentions and describes three kinds of baptism.

Our first window of insight comes through John the Baptist, who declared,

As for me, *I baptize you with water for repentance*, but He who is coming after me is mightier than I, and I am not fit to remove His sandals; *He will baptize you with the Holy Spirit* and fire.

Matthew 3:11, emphasis added

John's baptism for repentance represented the Old Covenant. Jesus' baptism with the Holy Spirit represents the New Covenant. It would not be fully realized, however, until the outpouring of the Holy Spirit on Pentecost, following His death and resurrection. When Jesus presented Himself for baptism at the age of thirty, not only did this experience launch His three years of public ministry, but it also gave us a window into the deeper meaning of the baptism that was about to be revealed. Scripture reports:

After being baptized, Jesus came up immediately from the water; and behold, the heavens were opened, and he saw the Spirit of God descending as a dove and lighting on Him, and behold, a voice out of the heavens said, "This is My beloved Son, in whom I am well pleased."

Matthew 3:16–17

Here we see the affirmation of the Father, "This is my beloved Son." And we see a "power encounter" as the Holy Spirit descends upon Jesus and immediately leads Him into the wilderness, where He is victorious over Satan's temptations during a forty-day fast (see Matthew 4:1–11). Then He returns in the fullness of the Spirit to recruit His first disciples and begin His three years of public ministry.

Jesus' baptism represents a transition point between the Old and the New Covenants, and it constitutes a teachable moment for us today as we endeavor to rediscover His Ekklesia. We can clearly see that New Testament baptism is meant to be a power encounter that connects the love of God, the life of Jesus and the power of the Holy Spirit in us, to propel us forward as newly admitted members of the Ekklesia. I emphasize in this session's *Ekklesia* chapter how the Spirit is responsible for everything pertaining to the new life:

. . . for our salvation, for leading us, for empowering us to overcome fear, for intimacy to address God as Father, and for assuring us of our eternal inheritance. Wow! Death of the old nature is wonderful, but without the new life of the Spirit, the message becomes focused on the stick of death without the carrot of new life.

Share: Did you notice the presence of the Trinity—the Father, Son and Holy Spirit—in the story of Jesus' baptism? What role does each member play?

_____

_____

_____

Deeper: If you have a church background, share your understanding of the meaning and emphasis attached to water baptism by your local congregation or denomination. Is it accompanied by the power encounter described above?

Read: Jesus confirmed this transition from the Old Covenant to the New Covenant on several different occasions. For example, on the last day of the feast at the Temple, He declared,

> He who believes in Me, as the Scripture said, "From His innermost being will flow rivers of living water." But this *He spoke of the Spirit*, whom those who believed in Him were to receive; for the Spirit was not yet given, because Jesus was not yet glorified.
>
> John 7:38–39, emphasis added

And following His resurrection from the dead, Jesus met with His disciples and told them to wait for what the Father had promised, which He had already told them about, "for John baptized with water, but you will be baptized with the Holy Spirit not many days from now'" (Acts 1:5).

On the Day of Pentecost, when the Holy Spirit descended on the disciples, Jesus' promises became reality. Empowered by the Spirit, the disciples took their first steps toward fulfilling the Great Commission. Peter preached the message of salvation, bridging from the Law and the Prophets to the Gospel of the Kingdom of God. The Bible describes what happened next:

> Now when they heard this, they were pierced to the heart, and said to Peter and the rest of the apostles, "Brethren, what shall we do?" Peter said to them, "*Repent, and each of you be baptized in the name of Jesus Christ* for the forgiveness of your sins; and *you will receive the gift of the Holy Spirit*. For the promise is for you and your children and for all who are far off, as many as the Lord our God will call to Himself."
>
> Acts 2:37–39, emphasis added

That day three thousand people believed, were baptized and were filled with the Holy Spirit . . . and the Ekklesia was born! Throughout chapter 9, I emphasize the fact that from the Day of Pentecost forward, New Testament water baptism is indelibly connected to receiving the gift of the Holy Spirit. In other words, water baptism and the baptism in the Holy Spirit were closely linked, not drawn out over time and experience.

As I said in *Ekklesia*, unfortunately today, the subject of the baptism in the Holy Spirit represents a major discordant issue between charismatic and more traditional believers, and it goes beyond speaking or not speaking in tongues. My goal here and in the book is to show "a more excellent biblical way" that hopefully will enable both camps to see the baptism by the Holy Spirit as a uniting, not a dividing, topic.

Share: On the basis of your personal experience and observation, why has the baptism in the Holy Spirit so often been a point of division rather than unity? Is this changing?

_____

_____

Read: In the book of Acts, we are able to observe the learning curve of the early Ekklesia as the first believers in Jesus came to understand the connection between personal faith, water baptism and baptism in the Holy Spirit.

Read (optional): For further background on the previous point, these examples from *Ekklesia* provide a brief but fascinating summary:

- Philip baptized new Samaritan converts in water "in the name of Jesus," signifying that they as non-Jews were acknowledging Him as the Messiah. When Peter and John arrived on their subsequent inspection tour, they "began laying their hands on them, and they were receiving the Holy Spirit" (Acts 8:17). In this case, water baptism preceded the baptism of the Holy Spirit.

- In the case of Saul's conversion experience, Acts 9:1–20 records that he was *first* filled with the Holy Spirit, and *then* was baptized in water. A few short days after that, he began proclaiming Jesus in the synagogues.

- Peter's experience speaking in Cornelius' home was equally unique in that the Holy Spirit of His own accord fell upon all those listening, with the evidence of "speaking with tongues," while Peter was still trying to explain Him (see Acts 10:44–48). The early Ekklesia was being "pushed" by the Holy Spirit to embrace new realities!

- Yet again, in Acts 19:1–7 Paul found new disciples in Ephesus who had been baptized "into John's baptism" but had not even heard that there was a Holy Spirit. Paul baptized them in the name of Jesus, and when he laid hands on them, the Holy Spirit came with the manifestation of tongues and prophesying. Again, the sequence was different, but the common denominator was the same: the evidential power and presence of the Holy Spirit.

Read: Regardless of the order of events, water baptism and baptism in the Holy Spirit were permanently intertwined in the narrative of the book of Acts. The key to seeing the symbiotic connection between these two baptisms is found in the need for every new believer to have a personal power encounter with the resurrected Jesus and experience the infilling of the Holy Spirit. This is not only necessary in order to experience new life in Christ; it is also imperative in order for us to become agents of transformation in the world as Jesus' Ekklesia. After I share my personal baptismal story in chapter 9 and the longing in my heart even as a youth for more of the presence and power of God, I conclude,

> The doctrinal split over the "baptism in the Holy Spirit" should no longer divide us. The power of the Word is in reality the work of the Spirit, the only One who convinces and leads us into all truth. The power of the Spirit is equally essential, and both camps need the strength that the other brings to the mix, because we all need the baptism of the Holy Spirit as described in the Word, to become like Jesus, who has only one Body.

Share: What role does the Holy Spirit play in your daily life right now? Try to describe it in very practical terms.

_____

_____

_____

_____

Deeper: What do you think Paul meant when he encouraged believers to "walk by the Spirit" and "keep in step with the Spirit" (Galatians 5:16; 25 NIV)?

_____

_____

How are your "steps" these days? Are you fully committed to letting the Holy Spirit guide them? Does He do it? What evidence do you have? Can you share it with your group?

_____

_____

_____

_____

Read: Why is the Church today so lacking in the power of the Holy Spirit, which, as we have seen, is absolutely essential to living a new life in Christ and having an impact on the world? In _Ekklesia_, I suggest that it is because we have confused wisdom with power. But look, for example, at the way the apostle Paul summarizes his message and strategy for sharing the Gospel: "But we preach Christ crucified . . . Christ the *power* of God and the *wisdom* of God" (1 Corinthians 1:23–24, emphasis added). Paul continues in the next chapter:

> For I determined to know nothing among you except Jesus Christ, and Him crucified. . . . and my message and my preaching were *not in persuasive words of wisdom*, but in *demonstration of the Spirit and of power*, so that your faith would not rest on the *wisdom of men, but on the power of God.*
>
> 1 Corinthians 2:2–5, emphasis added

I note in *Ekklesia* that the order of the words *power* and *wisdom* is very important in these verses, just like the order of numbers in a mathematical equation. Why?

_____

_____

We observe in Scripture that most of the first believers in Jesus converted to Christianity not because they came to understand Jesus mentally, but because they had a power encounter with Him and then grew in wisdom through His teachings. This was definitely Paul's experience on the road to Damascus.

In the Church today this order is often reversed, to our detriment. Water baptism is too often administered as a religious ceremony after several informative classes, while the importance of the baptism of the Holy Spirit (a personal power encounter) is often missing at that point in time (whereas in the New Testament, the two were inseparably linked). This is why I conclude at the end of chapter 9,

> Rather than leading new believers to come into contact with the power of the cross and the resurrection in a supernatural way, we inform them about such power and get them on a journey to find it. As a result, they end up *convinced* rather than *converted*. Baptizing them in such a state—without them having experienced the "power of the Holy Spirit"—may qualify them as members of a local fellowship, but they will not be transformational members of His Ekklesia.

Share: Does my statement from the book ring true with your observation of the Church today? How so? Where are you in this journey?

_____

_____

_____

_____

Deeper: Who will be more motivated to reach out to the world, someone who is *convinced* or someone who is *converted* through a genuine power encounter with God? Why?

_____

_____

Read: What happens when we dichotomize the Word and the Holy Spirit's manifestations? Quite candidly, as I say in *Ekklesia*, I dare to suggest that by allowing this unscriptural division, we have succumbed to a "less excellent way" where faulty positions cause the center to cave in. And taken to an extreme, as a result we may see manifestations not rooted in the Word, or we may hear the Word preached without any confirming signs. The former leaves us stranded in "emotion-land," and the latter in "intellectual-land." God has created us with both a brain and a heart, so we must do all we can to guard against this damaging dichotomy.

Share: What will it take in the Ekklesia today to claim the "more excellent way," embracing both the Word and the Holy Spirit, and thereby moving baptism from what is all too often merely a "religious ceremony" to a life-giving "power encounter"? Have you experienced the "baptism in the Holy Spirit" in your life?

_____

_____

_____

Session Summary

- In the Great Commission of Matthew 28:16–20, Jesus not only tells His disciples to go and make disciples of all nations; He also instructs His followers to baptize the nations.
- New Testament water baptism is meant to be the result of a "power encounter," orchestrated by the baptism in the Holy Spirit, that connects the love of God, the life of Jesus and the power of the Holy Spirit, propelling us forward as members of the Ekklesia.
- When it comes to baptism as practiced today, it is helpful to see the strength that other churches, denominations, theologies and practices bring to the table, so that together we can find a "more excellent biblical way."
- The Ekklesia today must reclaim water baptism from a "religious ceremony" to a "power encounter" by rediscovering its linkage to baptism in the Holy Spirit, so that people are not just *convinced*, but are *converted*.

Transformed Living

Read: Your **Personal Life Application** this week is to write a note to someone who "speaks peace" in your city or region. Offer this person some words of appreciation and encouragement for his or her efforts to "seek and save that which was lost." Also offer to do this person a favor that puts the *real* Jesus on display by responding to his or her felt needs. Focus on someone outside the traditional evangelistic ministries of the Church—someone working in the marketplace in business, education or government (including law enforcement), or someone serving through a community organization. Offer to do something for the person that meets a felt need in him or her and puts the *real* Jesus on display. This application is a simple example of how the principles of prayer evangelism can be a blessing to our cities and nations when we make them our lifestyle.

Your **Group Application** this week is twofold:

1. Sign up for "Transformation on Demand" at www. transformour world.org, which will allow you to watch transformation documentaries and access other instructional material. In this group study of *Ekklesia*, you will find these documentaries helpful as encouraging illustrations of transformation in progress. The online instructions to sign up are simple and self-guided.

2. Watch the *Transformation in Brantford, Canada* documentary as a group or individually (as time allows). In this video you will meet Pastor Brian Beattie, who shares how their local congregation had a telling impact on their city by first taking the Kingdom of God to where the Gates of Hades were entrenched in the marketplace. They then led people into the Kingdom in the marketplace and offered baptisms in the public square. Here is a transformation church that has reclaimed baptism from a "religious ceremony" to a "power encounter." It is an awesome testimony of the Ekklesia in action.

As you watch the video, reflect on the following questions and take some notes. What did the members of this Ekklesia do to get out of the four walls of the Church and positively affect their community? What were the felt needs to which they responded? How did the public baptisms become symbolic of what they did for the whole city?

Ekklesia Prayer and Ministry

Take a few minutes to share personal prayer requests for yourself and others, or share situations in your church, business, school or community that are on your heart. As time allows, close with a period of Spirit-led prayer and ministry to one another. You can jot down the prayer requests here to help you remember them:

_____

_____

_____

_____

_____

Reading Assignment

In preparation for Session 8, read chapters 10 and 11 in *Ekklesia*, "A New Understanding of Baptizing Nations" and "A Fuller Understanding of *How* to Baptize a Nation."

Daily Devotions

Read: Read and reflect on the passages that follow, and continue to pray and seek that personal power encounter with the Holy Spirit that we have been talking about during this session. May God's richest blessings fall upon you!

Day One—1 John 4:7–12

In what ways does God's love compel you to love others? Which verse in today's passage is similar to John 3:16, "For God so loved the world, that He gave His only begotten Son, that whoever believes in Him shall not perish, but have eternal life"? Reflect on ways that you would like to see God's love become more complete and more perfected in you.

Day Two—Ephesians 1:15–23

As you read this Scripture and reflect on it, ask God to give you "a spirit of wisdom and of revelation in the knowledge of Him" (verse 17). Then pray that "the eyes of your heart may be enlightened" (verse 18). According to verse 22, who is the Head of the Ekklesia?

Day Three—Acts 9:1–19

Whom do you observe in society today "breathing threats" against Christians? Reflect on your conversion experience. Did God have to knock you down before He could pick you up? In verse 17, what did Ananias tell Saul that God had sent him to do for him? What took place in verse 18 right after Saul's eyes were opened?

Day Four—Galatians 3:23–29

Paul says that the Law became our teacher until faith could be revealed. What kind of clothing does verse 27 say that we have received as a result of being "baptized into Christ"? Verse 28 is one of the most profound statements of unity in Christ found in the Bible. How does this verse speak to the divisions you see in society today?

Day Five—John 14:25–27

Depending on your Bible translation, in verse 25 Jesus calls the Holy Spirit an Advocate or Helper. What does this role of the Holy Spirit mean to you? We see that the Holy Spirit is also a teacher, because Jesus says that the Spirit will "teach you all things, and bring to your remembrance all that I said to you" (verse 26). How do these roles of the Holy Spirit contribute to the peace that Jesus describes in verse 27?

Day Six—Romans 6:1–7

Are you clinging to any sins in your life on the basis of a false confidence that Jesus will forgive you no matter what? What does Paul say about this attitude in verses 1–2? How does this linkage between baptism and the death and resurrection of Jesus Christ speak to the power encounter that baptism is meant to bring? What does it mean to you to "walk in newness of life," as verse 4 says?

Day Seven—your eGroup meets today! Enjoy!

SESSION 8

What this lesson is about:

If the Great Commission in Matthew 28:18–20 is about discipling nations, then it is also about "baptizing" nations. How are we to go about that? A study of the Greek word *baptizontes* and the key to its meaning, which comes straight from a pickle jar, will show us how. "Baptizing" a city or a nation is a process that begins with an event and continues by progressively saturating it with the teachings of Jesus to improve its status.

What you will walk away with:

You will see that in the same way as the baptism of the Holy Spirit starts a process of sanctification in us by which we are progressively transformed into the image of God's Son, so it is with discipling and baptizing a nation. It begins when any part of a city or nation is first exposed to and impacted by the Spirit, usually through an eye-opening miracle or power encounter that validates with righteous deeds the proclamation of the Gospel of the Kingdom. The city or nation is then progressively submerged in the teachings of Jesus. You will also learn how Jesus has empowered you as part of His Ekklesia to play a key role in this process.

Sharing Life

Watch: Play the video introduction for Session 8. This session is based on chapters 10 and 11 in *Ekklesia*, "A New Understanding of Baptizing Nations" and "A Fuller Understanding of *How* to Baptize a Nation."

Pray Together: Dear heavenly Father, thank You for promising to be with us and to be our Teacher as we continue our rediscovery of the Church that Jesus is building, His Ekklesia. As we go deeper into Your Word today, we ask that Your Holy Spirit open our hearts and minds to greater revelation and illumination, for the sake of "loving the world and being the Church" that You have commissioned us to be. In Jesus' name, Amen.

Read: Begin this session by reviewing your **Life Applications** from Session 7.

Share: Your **Personal Life Application** this past week was to write a personal note of encouragement to a marketplace minister in your city or region who is committed to "seek and save that which was lost." You were also to offer to do this person a favor that puts the *real* Jesus on display by responding to his or her felt needs. If it does not need to remain confidential, whom did you send a note to? How did you offer to help? Have you received a response? You may choose to follow up with a phone call or personal visit so that you can continue implementing the principles of prayer evangelism in your city.

Your **Group Application** was to watch the transformation video *Transformation in Brantford, Canada*. This local Ekklesia, led by Pastor Brian Beattie, is amazingly loving and creative in its approaches to reaching the city of Brantford for Jesus. What touched you the most about the baptisms in Brantford's public square? What felt needs did the Ekklesia respond to in the city? And how are the Ekklesia's members in effect baptizing the whole city?

_____

_____

_____

_____

_____

Transformed Thinking

Read: As I introduced in the previous session, the key to understanding the concept of baptizing a nation is not to focus on the method or the means, but rather to focus on the nature of baptism and its desired outcome.

In Matthew 28:19, where Jesus says, "Go therefore and make disciples of all the nations, *baptizing them* in the name of the Father and the Son and the Holy Spirit" (emphasis added), the word *them* refers to the subject that precedes it, *nations*. Furthermore, the Greek word translated "baptizing" is the adjectival participle, *baptizontes*. This participle is derived from two other Greek words: *bapto* and *baptizo*.

This is where it gets interesting, because the meaning of these two words illustrates the fullness of the transformation process that is involved in baptizing both individuals and nations. *Bapto* means "to dip, to immerse," and *baptizo* means "to submerge (as in a sunken vessel)," a process that results in a permanent change of state or condition. (You can reread the first few paragraphs of chapter 10 in the book for a quick refresher about these words.)

The parallels between the baptism of individuals and nations are self-evident. Christian baptism begins with *bapto*, an initial dipping or immersion, which leads to *baptizo*, an ongoing submersion in the teachings of Jesus and the power of the Holy Spirit, which produces a permanent life change.

The process by which a cucumber becomes a pickle, discovered in a recipe that predates Jesus' time on earth by about two hundred years, provides a very visual example of this. Nicander's ancient description of the pickling process, which I included near the start of chapter 10, uses both Greek words. In order to make a pickle, a cucumber must first be "dipped" (*bapto*) in boiling water and then "immersed" (*baptizo*) in a vinegar solution. The first part of this process is temporary and leads to a softening of the skin. The second part of this process is long-term and results in a permanent change. As I say in the book, "This is why in the case of an individual, the initial power encounter (*bapto*) by the Holy Spirit must be followed by a permanent submersion (*baptizo*) in the Word (the teachings of Jesus). The same is true for nations."

Share: Has anyone in your group ever made pickles? If so, have the person explain to the group in his or her own words the process described above.

Deeper: Is it possible that many Christians today have received the *bapto* but not the *baptizo*? Or perhaps the opposite? What might be the evidence?

_____

_____

Read: Unfortunately, the English word *baptizing* that appears early in the Great Commission does not capture the full intent of the Greek words that underlie it, unless it is intimately connected to the phrases that follow it in Jesus' instructions. Read Matthew 28:19–20 (emphasis added) once again:

> Go therefore and make disciples of all the nations, *baptizing* them *in the name of* the Father and the Son and the Holy Spirit, *teaching them to observe all* that I commanded you; and lo, *I am with you always*, even to the end of the age.

A nation is being baptized first when its totality, or any part of it, is exposed to and affected by the Spirit, usually through an eye-opening miracle or power encounter that validates the proclamation with righteous deeds. Then the nation comes under divine authority and reflects the character of the Triune God: the Father, Son and Holy Spirit. It is being baptized second when it is introduced to a process of permanent change that results from being completely submerged in the teachings of Jesus and observing them as a way of life. The power that undergirds this whole process, as

I noted in an earlier session, is the authority of Jesus and the promise of His presence with us always.

The key insight here is that baptizing, as connected with making disciples of nations, is not a religious ceremony or a one-time event, which is how we tend to think of it. Rather, it is a process that leads to permanent change. In chapter 10 I put it this way: "The 'pickling' (*baptizontes*) of our own heart is a process of submersion in the Word that becomes complete over time. In the same way, when the Kingdom of God infuses a nation, a similar process for societal transformation is set in motion."

Share: How can you be more effective in helping people become fully immersed in the character of God, the teachings of Jesus and the accompanying manifestations (evidence) of the Holy Spirit? Inside the four walls of the Church? In your community?

_____

_____

_____

_____

Deeper: How would you describe yourself in the baptism process? Newly dipped, fully immersed or somewhere in between? Sour or sweet? Crunchy or juicy?

_____

_____

Read: In chapter 10 of *Ekklesia*, I talk about two inspiring examples that illustrate the practical implementation of this new understanding of baptizing nations. The first involves the Ling Ying Public Primary School, a village school on the border between Hong Kong and China. The *bapto*, or initial dipping process, took place when the school principal, joined by other transformation-minded leaders, dedicated the school to the Lord. The *baptizo* occurred as the teachers were taught transformation paradigms and principles. The culture of the school began to change from one of discouragement to encouragement, and from low achievement to outstanding achievement. This led to expanded facilities and public recognition by the secretary of education for Hong Kong.

This full immersion process continues to this day as Kingdom values are being infused into the culture of the school, and the world is taking notice. Many students have come to know Jesus, and teachers are ministering to them with love and the principles of prayer evangelism.

Share: What is the infusion of hope that is most needed in the school that your children attend? Or in the school system in your area?

_____

_____

Deeper: What practical steps could you take to *bapto* and *baptizo* your schools?

_____

_____

_____

Read: The continuing story of transformation in Ciudad Juárez, Mexico, serves as another outstanding example of a nation being baptized. When Pastors Poncho Murguía and Brian Burton stood on a hill overlooking the city during the height of violence and adopted the city in prayer, it was a *bapto* of sorts. They were spiritually "dipping the city" into the love and promises of God.

But that was just the start. The *baptizo*, or full immersion, of the city in the teachings of Jesus continues through dozens of transformation initiatives touching every facet of society. I highlighted two of them in chapter 11. Corruption is being uprooted through a program sanctioned by the government called *Avanza sin Tranza*—"Thrive without Bribes." The teachings of Jesus are being presented in secular language through a twelve-lesson coaching program based on biblical principles. Hundreds of "influencers" have signed on, and the culture of bribery is being changed to reflect "righteousness and peace and joy in the Holy Spirit."

A second *bapto* event took place when Poncho and his team adopted the worst public school in Juárez and began to intercede in prayer and to "bind and release" with the keys of the Kingdom Jesus gave His Ekklesia. The evil and corruption that had gripped this school were the epitome of the Gates of Hades. But a schoolwide assembly became the turning point when an anointed speaker led the students to repent for the blatant disrespect and abuse they had shown their teachers. Forgiveness opened the door to a total transformation.

Remarkably, the state sub-secretary of education has now given Poncho and his team one thousand schools to submerge, or *baptizo*, through a values curriculum that is based on the teachings of Jesus. It is also designed to equip students to "minister" to the needs of the city through activities that include caring for the elderly, repairing local homes, arranging medical assistance for the infirm and providing others with food and friendship. All of this is evidence that Ciudad Juárez is experiencing a *baptizo* in its schools, government and business institutions. It is going through a process by which the "cucumber" that yesterday was the murder capital of the world is now being progressively submerged in the transforming dye of God's Kingdom so that its status will be changed to the safest city in Mexico!

Share: If nations are going to be discipled, why is it important that we both *bapto* and *baptizo* them? How does the testimony of Ciudad Juárez illustrate this?

_____

_____

_____

_____

Deeper: Why is it important that the Ekklesia provide both prophetic acts that declare the promises of God (such as the adoption exercise done by Poncho and Brian over Ciudad Juárez) *and* practical solutions that incorporate the teachings of Jesus?

_____

_____

As I say at the end of chapter 10, all this leads us to a concluding question: Who does the baptizing of the nations? Here is my answer from the book:

> Who does the baptizing of the nations? The Ekklesia—which consists of believers like you and me. When and where do we do it? As we "go on our way," just as Barbara Chan, Pastor Wong, Michael Brown, King Flores, Poncho Murguía and Lydia, the businesswoman in Acts 16:14–15, have done. They opened the door of their city and nation through the proclamation of the Gospel of the Kingdom by deeds and actions (*bapto*) that set in motion a process of "submerging" them (*baptizo*), which has as its outcome putting the nations on course toward being discipled.

Session Summary

- Baptizing either an individual or a nation is meant to begin with a power encounter with the Holy Spirit that leads to a progressive submersion in the teachings of Jesus, which produces permanent change.
- Discipling a nation involves bringing the Kingdom of God to the nation's doorstep so that it will have an opportunity to enter into it.
- The process of baptizing a city or a nation begins when it is placed under the authority of the Triune God and is subsequently submerged in the teachings of Jesus.

- If this transformation can happen in places like Hong Kong and Ciudad Juárez, by God's grace and power, transformation can happen in your city!

Transformed Living

Read: Your **Personal Life Application** this week is to ask the Holy Spirit to take you from *bapto* to *baptizo*—in other words, from dipping to dripping. This can happen in a number of ways, but here are a couple of suggestions:

- If you have never been water baptized, consider how you might be baptized.
- God is eager to give you a fresh anointing of His presence and power through the Holy Spirit. This is an important step in your Ekklesia journey.
- If you are still seeking God but are uncertain about your relationship with Him, seek the counsel and encouragement of those around you. God loves you and is more than patient with you. He is eager to welcome you into His Ekklesia.

Your **Group Life Application** is to consider how you can both *bapto* and *baptizo* your city, "a la Ciudad Juárez" and the other testimonies that I have shared. Reflect on this application by returning to the specific issue, or unreconciled social gap, that your group has been responding to in previous sessions. What did you do regarding that social gap to put deeds to your words? In all likelihood, your actions as a group already represent a *bapto*. You have already dipped hurting people into the love and kindness of the Lord. How can you build on these good works in light of this deeper teaching today, so that your dipping becomes a full-immersion dripping, or *baptizo*, in the teachings of Jesus and in the power of the Holy Spirit to see the character of God developed in you? Talk about it now and jot down some thoughts:

_____

_____

_____

_____

After you arrive at some insights, once again develop an action plan that outlines at least a few next steps that will keep you moving forward in loving your city as Jesus loves it. This is what it means to be the Ekklesia, God's instrument for global transformation. Also take your action plan to the Lord in prayer during the upcoming group ministry time.

Ekklesia Prayer and Ministry

Take time right now to share prayer requests, needs, updates and testimonies before you pray together. As time allows, close with a period of Spirit-led prayer and ministry to one another. You can jot down the prayer requests here to help you remember them:

_____

_____

_____

_____

_____

Reading Assignment

In preparation for Session 9, read chapters 12 and 13 in *Ekklesia*, "A Fuller Understanding of the Ekklesia's Social Agenda" and "A Fuller Understanding of the Incarnation."

Daily Devotions

Read: Be blessed with another week of daily devotions as God continues to change you from a cucumber to a Kingdom-minded pickle.

Day One—2 Corinthians 5:14–6:2

Because the love of Christ controls us, whom does verse 15 say we are to live for? When you became a new creation in Christ, what "old things" passed away and what "new things" became a part of your life? What is the ministry of reconciliation that we have been given as "ambassadors for Christ" (verses 18–20)? How do the first two verses of 2 Corinthians 6 foster a sense of urgency in the Ekklesia today?

Day Two—James 1:19–27

How will the qualities James describes, like being "quick to hear, slow to speak and slow to anger" in verse 19, serve you well as you reach out to your family, neighbors, co-workers, classmates and others? Someone once said, "Vision without action is only delusion." In light of verse 22, do you think James would agree? In verse 25, are you a "forgetful hearer" or an "effectual doer"? How does James describe pure and undefiled religion in verse 27?

Day Three—Psalm 133:1–3

How does this beautiful psalm speak to the issue of unity in the Body of Christ, for the sake of mission to the world? According to the psalmist, what is the connection between unity and blessing? When the Lord commands a blessing, what does it lead to?

Day Four—Ephesians 4:1–16

What are the qualities in verses 1–3 that Paul says should characterize the way we represent the Lord? There are seven "ones" in verses 4–6 that represent verse 3's "unity of the Spirit in the bond of peace." What are they? What is the special role given to apostles, prophets, evangelists, pastors and teachers, as described in verses 12–13? Now look at verses 15–16. What does "speaking the truth in love" have to do with growing up in Christ?

Day Five—1 John 3:1–18

There is no greater blessing than being called a child of God. What warning does John give in verse 7? According to verse 8, for what purpose did the Son of God appear? How does verse 18 summarize our call to serve the world in Jesus' name?

Day Six—Revelation 3:7–22

Contrast the message of Jesus to the Ekklesia in Philadelphia with His message to the Ekklesia in Laodicea. What is promised to both? If Jesus were to knock on the door of your heart today, in what part of your life do you still need to make room so that you can welcome Him in? What door might Jesus be knocking on in your city?

Day Seven—your eGroup meets today! Be blessed!

SESSION 9

The first-century Ekklesia introduced a radical and revolutionary social agenda that launched a process that literally changed the world. With the subsequent institutionalization of the Church, however, what was a lifestyle before that implemented Jesus' agenda became programs of good deeds that fall short of transforming society. But Jesus belongs more in the marketplace than in a monastery, because He was *fully* incarnated into the affairs of the world and its institutions.

The Ekklesia must never forsake the assembling of its members for the training and encouragement that the writer to the Hebrews speaks of (see Hebrews 10:25). Yet you will clearly see that Jesus has given us the keys to open and shut gates for Him to come into human hearts, cities and nations. We are not dealing with a hostile audience, "for the anxious longing of the creation waits eagerly for the revealing of the sons of God. . . . For we know that the whole creation groans and suffers the pains of childbirth together until now" (Romans 8:19, 22). The key is that the Jesus whom we put on display in the marketplace must be the real Jesus.

Sharing Life

Watch: Play the video introduction for Session 9. This session is based on chapters 12 and 13 in *Ekklesia*, "A Fuller Understanding of the Ekklesia's Social Agenda" and "A Fuller Understanding of the Incarnation."

Pray Together: Dear heavenly Father, thank You for promising to be with us and to be our Teacher as we continue our rediscovery of the Church that Jesus is building, His Ekklesia. As we go deeper into Your Word today, we ask that Your Holy Spirit open our hearts and minds to greater revelation and illumination, for the sake of our loving the world and becoming the Ekklesia. We also ask that You supernaturally open our spiritual eyes so that we can gain a fuller understanding of the incarnation and see the *real*

Jesus. Inspire and empower us to identify with the world, to stand in the gap and to offer salvation to the world as His Ekklesia. In Jesus' name, Amen.

Read: Begin this session by reviewing your **Life Applications** from Session 8.

Share: Your **Personal Life Application** this past week was to ask the Holy Spirit to take you from *bapto* to *baptizo*, or in other words, from dipping to a complete submersion. I suggested three options: water baptism for those who have never been water baptized; prayer for full immersion or a fresh baptism in the Holy Spirit; or seeking counsel and encouragement from others, if you need it, regarding your relationship with Jesus. Did you choose one of these options? If so, where are you in this process? Share this with your eGroup now.

Your **Group Life Application** was to consider how you can both *bapto* and *baptizo* your city, "a la Ciudad Juárez" and the other testimonies that I have shared. You were also to reflect on the specific issue, or unreconciled social gap, that you began to respond to in previous sessions. Did you take any new action steps this week related to this application, steps that could begin to take individuals or groups or your whole city from *bapto* to *baptizo*, or from dipping to dripping, in the character of God, the teaching of Jesus and the power of the Holy Spirit? Discuss your progress and continue seeking the Lord for the next steps your group will take together.

Transformed Thinking

Read: The first-century Ekklesia embraced the words of Jesus from the Lord's Prayer when they were instructed to pray: "Your kingdom come. Your will be done, on earth as it is in heaven" (Matthew 6:10). As a result, they preached the full message of the Gospel of the Kingdom, having the expectation of seeing accompanying signs and wonders from heaven and social justice here on earth. As I stated at the beginning of chapter 12, Jesus' Ekklesia was never meant to be so heavenly minded as to become earthly irrelevant. On the contrary! It is a spiritual entity vested with governmental jurisdiction on earth to change world systems for the better. Jesus' teachings about social issues constitute what is known today as Christian ethics, and three major social evils that the Ekklesia is empowered to address stand out in His teachings: systemic poverty, slavery and the demeaning treatment of women.

Share: What is a quality that you perceive exists in heaven that you would like to see more of here on earth?

_____

_____

Read: Jesus began His public ministry by announcing "good news to the poor" (Luke 4:18 NIV). Later, we see that care for the poor became a hallmark of the Ekklesia: "For there was not a needy person among them" (Acts 4:34). How many needy persons were among them? Not one! Everyone's needs were met.

To achieve this same result in society today, we must deal with systemic poverty—the systems and structures that hold people in bondage. Poverty is not just one-dimensional (material). Rather, there are four dimensions of poverty evident in the Lord's Prayer:

- *Spiritual poverty*—afflicts those who don't know that God is their Father.
- *Relational poverty*—afflicts those whose focus is on themselves at the expense of the community to which they belong.
- *Motivational poverty*—afflicts those who have no adequate way or means or the confidence to tackle tomorrow's challenges.
- *Material poverty*—afflicts those who lack the resources necessary to sustain life.

Share: In what ways does your local church, business or organization respond to these four dimensions of poverty? What have the results been?

_____

_____

_____

_____

Why is it easier—although not necessarily the most effective—to focus primarily on material poverty? Why is it necessary for the traditionally rich and the traditionally poor to partner as peers in order to eliminate systemic poverty?

_____

_____

_____

_____

Deeper: Which of these four dimensions of poverty do you think is most impacting your community today? Why should these four dimensions be tackled together and not piece by piece?

Read: The early Ekklesia made a consistent commitment to both saving souls and the betterment of society. Yet eliminating systemic poverty was not the driver for the Ekklesia's mission; rather, it was evidence that Jesus Christ was alive in their midst. Why did significant numbers come to believe that Jesus was alive? Because, as I put it in chapter 12, apostolic witness of the *invisible* resurrection of Jesus Christ was made credible by *visible* radical transformation in the social arena.

We see how this transformation continued as the Ekklesia challenged the issue of slavery, a well-entrenched system in Jesus' day. His teaching provided the spiritual and ethical foundation for reformers who followed, including heroes like William Wilberforce, Abraham Lincoln, Mahatma Gandhi, Nelson Mandela and Martin Luther King Jr.

Jesus and His disciples taught that:

- Work is to be done as though doing it for the Lord (see Colossians 3:23).
- A worker is worthy of his or her wage (see 1 Timothy 5:18).
- Every person has equal access to the love and grace of God, regardless of his or her social or economic standing in life (see the book of Philemon).
- The rich and poor, owners and employees, have complementary gifts that are needed to break the stranglehold of systemic poverty in its four dimensions.

It is the concept of a righteous God, after all, that gave birth to moral absolutes that allow for social justice to triumph over systemic evil and that replace the evil with values and virtues.

Share: What are some manifestations of slavery that continue to exist in the world today? How can the Ekklesia both speak up and take effective action regarding this issue?

Deeper: How can employers and employees partner together to create more God-honoring, peaceful and equitable workplace environments?

_____

_____

Read: The third major social evil that Jesus tackled, and that His disciples continued to pursue, was discrimination against women, which resulted in social indenture. The social standing of women in Jesus' culture amounted to another form of slavery. In Galatians 3:28 (emphasis added), however, the apostle Paul made this paradigm-shifting declaration: "There is neither Jew nor Greek, there is neither slave nor free man, there is *neither male nor female*; for you are all one in Christ Jesus." The early Ekklesia lived out this theology in practice. Both Jesus and His apostles included women on their "ministry teams," and they treated women with honor and respect as equal partners before the Lord.

Jesus frequently extended grace to women whom society saw as worthless, as in the case of the woman caught in adultery in John 8. His approach, even in silence, brought accountability to those men who were tempted to cast the first stone at her. He also upheld the sanctity of marriage, challenging the callous attitude of the Jewish religious leaders who were quick to write certificates of divorce that left their discarded wives as social pariahs.

The apostle Paul extended this teaching about women even further when he instructed husbands and wives to "be subject to one another in the fear of Christ," treating one another with mutual love and respect, humility and service (Ephesians 5:21). This was radical stuff! As I note in chapter 12,

> . . . this restorative process went beyond the kitchen table and the bedroom. As full-fledged members of the Ekklesia, women in the New Testament were permitted and encouraged to participate in meetings, do public good works and receive teaching in the same manner and environment in which men had been taught in the Old Testament.

This set the stage for the fourth major focus of the Ekklesia: the restoration of the family by bringing salvation to the "oikos."

Share: How would you evaluate the quality of relationships that exist in your culture today between men and women, husbands and wives? What is the core value or spirit that must prevail for these quality relationships to exist in the home?

_____

_____

_____

_____

Deeper: Give some examples of where the Ekklesia still needs to speak and practice biblical truth regarding the treatment of women and the restoration of families.

_____

_____

Read: The apostle Paul experienced a revealing personal learning curve regarding the Ekklesia's social agenda that involved two major setbacks and two stunning setups for victory, both of which are very instructive for us today. I talk about these in more detail at the end of chapter 12, but I will review them briefly here.

Setback #1 occurred in Pisidian Antioch, a Roman colony. What began with the favor of the people and led to many believing in Jesus ended when "the Jews incited the devout women of prominence and the leading men of the city, and *instigated a persecution* against Paul and Barnabas, and drove them out of their district" (Acts 13:50, emphasis added).

Setback #2 took place in Thessalonica. Just as before, things started out great. Many believed, including God-fearing Greeks and some leading women. "But the Jews, becoming jealous and taking along some wicked men from the market place, formed a mob and *set the city in an uproar* . . . They stirred up the crowd and the city authorities" (Acts 17:5, 8, emphasis added). In both cases an Ekklesia was established, but the region was not transformed.

Setup #1 happened in Corinth, a bustling crossroads city of commerce, where Paul's ministry experienced a major breakthrough when a prominent leader named Crispus and his entire household were saved. During the next year and a half, Paul's preaching led to massive conversions. Once again, "the Jews with one accord *rose up against Paul* and brought him before the judgment seat" (Acts 18:12, emphasis added). This time, however, the local authorities rebuked Paul's adversaries, and the proconsul of Achaia "*drove them away from the judgment seat*" and dismissed the case (verse 16, emphasis added).

Setup #2 took place in Ephesus, where the move of God had a huge impact. The Scriptures record that "all who lived in Asia heard the word of the Lord, both Jews and Greeks," and "the word of the Lord was growing mightily and prevailing" (Acts 19:10, 20). Once again, opposition raised its ugly head: "About that time there occurred *no small disturbance* concerning the Way," and "The city *was filled with the confusion*, and they rushed with one accord into the theater, dragging along Gaius and Aristarchus, Paul's traveling companions from Macedonia" (verses 23, 29, emphasis added). Paul tried to come to their defense, but was prevented by the Asiarchs, high-ranking officials who are described as Paul's friends. Shortly afterward, this dicey encounter ended abruptly when the town clerk simply dismissed the mob. Case closed!

Why the setbacks that were such crushing defeats, followed by the setups that led to such great victories? Here is the observation I make in the book:

> Paul's identity, and that of his associates in the cities where the defeats took place, was religious. He was a preacher identified with the synagogue, an exclusivist religious body, whereas in Corinth and Ephesus he had moved his base of operations to the *marketplace*, which allowed him to become involved in the welfare of the city.

Paul's favor with the officials in Corinth and Ephesus was the result of doing favors for them. He had made it a point to help the poor, the hungry and the vulnerable, and these acts of kindness by his team had not gone unnoticed. The important takeaway is this: When Paul shifted his ministry emphasis from the synagogue to the marketplace, he became an asset to the cities he visited, even in the eyes of unbelievers. In these places he became known as a giver, not a taker. In his own words, Paul said:

> I have coveted no one's silver or gold or clothes. You yourselves know that these hands ministered to my own needs [as a tentmaker] and to the men who were with me. In everything I showed you that *by working hard in this manner you must help the weak* and remember the words of the Lord Jesus, that He Himself said, "It is more blessed to give than to receive."
>
> Acts 20:33–35, emphasis added

Share: Describe a favor that you or your local church could do that would contribute to the welfare of your city, as was the case with the apostle Paul.

_____

_____

_____

_____

Deeper: What setbacks have become setups as you have attempted to disciple your household, your place of work or perhaps your city for Jesus?

_____

_____

_____

_____

Read: The Ekklesia today is responding to the four dimensions of poverty with love, creativity and action empowered by the Holy Spirit. In the continuing story of Michael's Transportation Services in Vallejo, California, I tell you in chapter 12 about how Michael and Paulette Brown "sold down" instead of "selling up and out," making every employee a part owner and shareholder in their company. The haves and the have-nots became partners who shared their spiritual, relational, motivational and material wealth.

To break the cycle of systemic poverty, people need jobs, especially those people coming out of prison. Michael's Transportation Training Academy helps equip the formerly incarcerated with employable skills. Now, instead of an 80 percent recidivism rate among former inmates, there is a 100 percent job placement in the local community, which in turn gives these individuals a big leg up on a new and productive life.

In Brantford, Ontario, Freedom House, the Ekklesia led by Pastor Brian Beattie, has taken numerous steps to get outside the four walls and bless the city. As you saw in the Brantford video you watched in Session 7, its members clean up city parks and provide housing for homeless and needy families. They also serve free burgers (and fellowship) to the club crowd on Friday nights. During the winter they organize the city's annual Frosty Fest and put on a live Nativity scene at the request of city officials. In the summer they offer public baptisms—not in the church building, but in the city's public Harmony Square. To respond to another felt need, they share Kingdom values in the public schools through a superhero called Captain Kindness and a curriculum called "Superhero in Me."

As I say in *Ekklesia*,

> These testimonies exemplify the abilities that only the Ekklesia has. It can bridge the gender gap at home between spouses, between parents and children and between masters (owners) and slaves (employees) in the market-place. It can also integrate seamlessly the four dimensions of wealth— spiritual, relational, motivational and material—to tackle poverty, in order to disciple a city, a region and eventually a nation. At the very heart of these things is a rediscovery of the social agenda the first-century Ekklesia had, so that it can be carried on. This is crucial because when we do that, we will gain favor with everybody—rich and poor—but most importantly, with people in authority who can open or close doors for the Gospel to flow freely.

Share: Why is "doing favors for the people" so powerful for the Ekklesia? What makes it powerful?

Read: In chapter 13 of *Ekklesia*, I suggest that for the contemporary Church to succeed, it must first rediscover, and then learn to share with others, the "real Jesus." The obstacle to the world truly knowing the real Jesus is not in His character or recorded actions, since whatever else they believe about Him, most people agree that He was a good person who sacrificially cared for others. As I point out in my book, the main obstacle lies in people's perception that Jesus was an irrelevant hermit whose life and ethereal teachings made no contribution to solving the problems of society, and their perception that His followers have not done any better.

Share: Write down five things you think your nonbelieving friends or work associates might say if you asked them the question, "Who is Jesus?" Then compare notes with your eGroup. Which things are true? Which are false?

_____

_____

_____

_____

_____

Read: The key to getting to know the real Jesus is found in His incarnation, which is a central Christian teaching that states that God became flesh, assumed human nature and became a Man in the form of Jesus, the Christ. John 1:14 declares, "And the Word became flesh, and dwelt among us, and we saw His glory, glory as of the only begotten from the Father, full of grace and truth." Colossians 2:9 confirms, "For in Him [Christ] all the fullness of Deity dwells in bodily form."

To get to know the real Jesus, we must take a look at the record of His "real life," not just what people think they know about Him. Whom did He hang out with? How did He spend His time? What does His character reveal? How did He treat people? A scrutiny of the Scriptures reveals that Jesus was much more at home in the marketplace than in the synagogue. The following quick review of Jesus' life reveals some interesting facts:

- Jesus spent all but three years of His adult life as a carpenter in Nazareth, running a profitable business that His father had taught Him.
- Jesus' disciples all came from the marketplace and included professional fishermen, a doctor, a lawyer, a government tax collector and an accountant. No religious leaders were among the Twelve.
- The parables Jesus taught and the illustrations He used indicated a deep understanding of business principles and practices ranging from farming to venture capital.

- Most of Jesus' miracles took place in the marketplace of everyday life, including at a wedding, a funeral, in homes, in boats, on a hilltop, by the roadside and at a community watering hole.
- Jesus did the bulk of His teaching in nonreligious settings as He traveled from one town to the next, and as people gathered on a hillside or as He sat at a table with friends, enjoying food and drink.
- At a time when women and children were considered much inferior to men, Jesus validated their worth by welcoming children and including several women as friends and close ministry associates.
- Jesus demonstrated extraordinary compassion for the poor, the disabled, the diseased and the socially outcast.

I make the point in chapter 13 that Jesus was not just visiting the world, but was incarnated into it. He was therefore consistently able to affirm people who had no value in the opinion of their enemies or adversaries. For example,

- Jesus not only conversed with foreigners (those outside the Jewish faith); He also welcomed them into the Kingdom of God.
- Jesus challenged those in the religious establishment for their hypocrisy and challenged the governmental authorities for their pride and misuse of power.
- Following Jesus' return to heaven, the values and priorities that He taught continued in the lives of the apostles and members of the first-century Ekklesia. They were so committed to Him that they willingly gave their lives for the cause of the Gospel.

In these examples we see that even apart from Jesus' death and resurrection, His personal life and testimony offer great encouragement to the Ekklesia of today. To effectively and consistently have an impact on our world, we, too, must take the power and the presence of God that resides in the synagogue (the local church) into the marketplace, including the key arenas of business, education and government. We, too, must become known as "a friend of sinners" (see Matthew 11:19). We, too, must bridge the major social gaps in our culture, including racism, sexism, classism, denominationalism, poverty and injustice.

Share: How does the brief summary above of Jesus' lifestyle and priorities challenge many of the common misconceptions about Him? What kind of a Man was He really?

_____

_____

_____

_____

Deeper: In what ways was Jesus a radical within His culture? How is the Ekklesia called to be radical today?

_____

_____

_____

_____

What does it mean to you to be "the hands and feet of Jesus"?

_____

_____

Session Summary

- God's justice on earth is not complete until it becomes social justice, and social justice is impossible to achieve without the power of the Holy Spirit working through us.
- The early Ekklesia made a consistent commitment to both seeing people saved and contributing to the betterment of society.
- The elimination of systemic poverty in its four dimensions—spiritual, relational, motivational and material—is central to the message of the true Gospel, which always connects words with deeds.
- The equality and complementary roles of men and women begin in the home, but must extend to the Church and to the marketplace of everyday life.
- Every setback is a setup when we partner with God for transformation.
- When we do favors for our city, we find favor with our city.

Transformed Living

Read: The relationship between men and women, beginning with husbands and wives, is vital to the witness and ministry of the Ekklesia in the world. Your **Personal Life Application** this week involves a response to Jesus' social agenda, particularly to His honor and respect for women. Your assignment is straightforward: Find a special way to honor several of the women in your life, whether your spouse, your mother, a sister, a daughter or a spiritual mentor. Get creative. Apply the principles of prayer evangelism here as well. How can you "speak peace and bless" the women who have had an impact on your life? How can you strengthen your relationships, respond to these women's felt needs, pray for them and encourage them in the Lord?

Husbands, is it time for a special date? Dads, is it time to let your daughter know how much you love her? Women, is it time to honor that mother, sister or friend who has been there for you during tough times? Whom would you like to honor in some special way this week? Jot down their names here and go for it.

_____

_____

_____

_____

Your **Group Life Application** this week is to do a food and clothing drive (or a similar type of activity) within your local Ekklesia. (This could involve a number of eGroups working together.) Take whatever you collect to your local food bank or distribution center. You decide together what the most pressing needs are in your community and how you can rally others to join you in this cause. Also decide on the beginning and ending dates for your appeal. Select a point person for this project who is willing to run with it. Touch on the details here:

_____

_____

_____

_____

As you do this particular favor for your city, reflect further on the issue of systemic poverty and consider how you might respond to all four aspects— spiritual, relational, emotional and material—as you move forward into the future, when the Ekklesia in your area will address not just individual, but also systemic poverty.

Ekklesia Prayer and Ministry

Take time right now to share prayer requests, needs, updates and testimonies before you pray together. As time allows, close with a period of Spirit-led prayer and ministry to one another. Include prayers for those who are experiencing poverty in any of its forms. You can jot down the prayer requests here to help you remember them:

_____

_____

_____

_____

_____

Reading Assignment

In preparation for Session 10, read chapters 14 and 15 in *Ekklesia*, "A Fuller Understanding of What God Loves the Most" and "A Fuller Understanding of Spiritual Authority."

Daily Devotions

Read: The devotions this week will continue to provide you with opportunities to dig deeper into God's Word and apply it to your daily life. The Scriptures that follow build on the themes of the two *Ekklesia* chapters that we covered in this session.

Day One—Matthew 6:1–15

Note the strong counsel Jesus gives preceding the Lord's Prayer. What topics does He address? How does this teaching relate to how you respond to the issues of poverty in your community or how you do favors for your city? Are all prayers to be offered in private, or is there a deeper message?

Day Two—Luke 4:14–21

Why is it often toughest to minister in the place where you live? Why do you think that Jesus chose the words in verses 18–19, which are originally from Isaiah 61, to launch His public ministry? What do these words say about the real Jesus? How do these words parallel the four dimensions of systemic poverty? Who are the poor, the captives, the blind or the oppressed in your city?

Day Three—Luke 18:18–30

What was the "rich young ruler" lacking in his life? How is it that a person can be very religious, keeping all the rules, and still miss the mark? Is there anything that you can do to inherit eternal life (see Ephesians 2:8–10)? Is there an unhealthy attachment in your life that you are unwilling to let go of to follow Jesus? Ask God to set you free.

Day Four—John 4:1–26

Jesus' encounter with the Samaritan woman at Jacob's well speaks volumes about His treatment of women. What stands out to you? What is the "living water" He mentions in verse 10? How are the principles of prayer evangelism evident in His life and ministry to this woman? What did He mean in verse 23 when He told her that "true worshipers will worship the Father in spirit and truth"?

Day Five—Hebrews 4:14–16

How do these verses speak to Jesus' incarnation—that He was both 100 percent God and 100 percent Man? What does it mean to you to know that Jesus not only sympathizes with your weaknesses, but that He has been there, "tempted in all things as we are, yet without sin" (verse 15)? Why is Jesus described in verse 14 as a "great high priest"? Are you willing to respond to the invitation in verse 16 to "draw near with confidence" to Jesus today and receive mercy and grace in your time of need?

Day Six—Philemon 1:1–25

This New Testament letter is short but power packed. On what basis does Paul appeal to Philemon to receive the runaway slave, Onesimus? Note the phrases "my child . . . whom I have begotten," "sending my very heart" and "a beloved brother" (verses 10, 12, 16). How does this story illustrate the truth of Galatians 3:28? Who is an Onesimus in your life?

Day Seven—your eGroup meets today! Be blessed!

SESSION 10

What this lesson is about:

It may surprise you to hear that what God loves the most is not just the Ekklesia. And when we embrace everything that He loves, it radically changes for the better the way we see and do ministry as His Ekklesia. "Out-reach ministries" become "in-reach ministries" because the "congregation" just became citywide. With that in mind, we understand why Jesus invested His Ekklesia with the highest level of divine authority imaginable. We are to exercise that authority in ever-increasing concentric circles that begin with an initial and all-important point of inception.

What you will walk away with:

When you love what God loves—and He loves the world—then it makes sense to you that He would deploy qualified and skilled people like yourself into every aspect of the world to manifest His love. Once you understand this, it bestows on you a clear sense of legitimacy as you work in the marketplace. You will be able to see with biblical certainty that what you do there ministry-wise is not a footnote or an appendix, but the very essence of what God called you to be. Your point of inception is always key—no matter how small it might be. The stories I present in this session and the *Ekklesia* chapters it covers model for us powerful demonstrations of the impact of the ever-expanding concentric circles of authority that shatter the darkness in both the spiritual and natural realms.

Sharing Life

Watch: Play the video introduction for Session 10. This session is based on chapters 14 and 15 in *Ekklesia*, "A Fuller Understanding of What God Loves the Most" and "A Fuller Understanding of Spiritual Authority."

Pray Together: Dear heavenly Father, we bless You and praise Your name! Thank You for loving this world so much that You gave Your very best. Help us to walk in both grace and truth. Show us how to claim the spiritual authority You have given us and exercise it in the marketplace of everyday life so that Satan will fall down and Your Kingdom will grow. Show each of us where that point of inception is in our lives for Your light to begin to shatter the darkness. In Jesus' name, Amen.

Read: Begin this session by reviewing your **Life Applications** from Session 9.

Share: Your **Personal Life Application** this past week was to find a special way to honor several of the women in your life, whether your spouse, your mother, a sister, a daughter or a spiritual mentor. You were to implement the principles of prayer evangelism in expressing your appreciation for these women. Whom did you honor? Why? What did you do for them? Which steps of prayer evangelism did you incorporate?

_____

_____

_____

_____

Your **Group Life Application** this week was to organize a food and clothing drive (or some similar type of activity) within your local Ekklesia (possibly including other eGroups) and do a favor for your city on a group level. What did you do? Has the invitation to do this favor for your city inspired others to get on board? What is yet left to be done?

_____

_____

_____

Transformed Thinking

Read: In John 3:16, which could effectively serve as a summary of the whole Bible, Jesus declared, "For God *so loved the world*, that He gave His only begotten Son, that whoever believes in Him shall not perish, but have eternal life" (emphasis added).

What does God love? The world. How much does He love it? So much that He gave His very own Son. Yes, God loves the Church, too, because it is the Body of Christ and Jesus is the Head. The Ekklesia has a specific purpose and function, however, that it must clearly understand, or it will continue to turn inward. While Christ "loved the church and gave Himself up for her" (Ephesians 5:25), that same Church is a result of His love for the world.

That is why Jesus continued in John 3:17, "For God did not send the Son into the world to judge the world, but that *the world might be saved through Him*" (emphasis added). For that reason, I state near the beginning of chapter 14, "Surely God loved, loves and will forever love the world. This is why it is absolutely essential for us to love what God loves so much—the world."

Share: How would you rate yourself on the subject of "loving what God loves the most"? What things do you love instead?

_____

_____

Read: How is it that God can love people who reject Him every day and are so full of sin, pride, bitterness and anger? The answer, we read, is that God does not see people as they are now. He sees them as they "will be" when they come to Christ and are fully forgiven and restored. For us, that means a biblical shift in paradigm is necessary if we are to look at the world in a loving way. We must see it as "already" redeemed. Paul described how he saw people struggling with sin this way: "Therefore from now on we recognize no one according to the flesh" (2 Corinthians 5:16).

In order for us to truly love the world around us, the love of Christ must control us. Why? Because God has a bigger plan. Remember, the Great Commission has both an individual and a corporate mandate. After Paul's uplifting declaration in 2 Corinthians 5:17, "if anyone is in Christ, he is a new creature," he continues:

> Now all these things are from God, who reconciled us to Himself through Christ and gave us the *ministry of reconciliation*, namely, that God was in Christ reconciling the world to Himself, not counting their trespasses against them, and He has committed to us the word of reconciliation.
> Therefore, we are *ambassadors for Christ . . .*
>
> Verses 18–20, emphasis added

You may recall this humorous statement I make in the book: "If our favorite dish is barbecued lamb, God will not send us after a lost sheep. He knows that when we find it, we will eat it!" Then I explain, "In essence, we must become incarnated in the world the way Jesus was, to be its friend and attain the highest level of love Jesus described: 'Greater love has no one than this, that one lay down his life for his friends' (John 15:13)."

Share: What are the role and authority of an ambassador?

_____

_____

How does this parallel our role and authority as members of Jesus' Ekklesia?

_____

_____

Read: To love the world the way God loves it, we must approach it as Jesus did, with both grace and truth. John 1:14 says, "And the Word became flesh, and dwelt among us, and we saw His glory . . . full of grace and truth." I describe this in *Ekklesia* as a "binary truth." To achieve the desired result, we must exercise both of these qualities, grace and truth, in the proper order and balance. If we offer only grace, we become nothing more than motivational speakers presenting "feel-good Christianity." If we offer only truth, it is easy to become arrogant and judgmental. We may be right, but sinners will experience rejection rather than love and turn a deaf ear. With this binary truth, both qualities are needed in full measure to reach the world in Jesus' name, because "the kindness of God leads you to repentance" (Romans 2:4).

Share: Have you ever had a negative experience trying to "witness" to someone? What do you think was missing in the exchange?

_____

_____

Deeper: What is different about the approach that Jesus teaches in Luke 10, which we call prayer evangelism?

_____

_____

Read: To become Jesus' Ekklesia today, I suggest in the book that we must stop defining the good things we do for Jesus *beyond* the walls of our local congregation as "outreach ministries." Instead, we must recognize that our congregation includes all the people in the city, not just our church members. Then former "out-reaches" become "in-reaches" because the Ekklesia is present and invested in society.

This paradigm shift will cause us to fully embrace our calling as marketplace ministers. We will no longer perceive "church" as what we do in a building for an hour on a Sunday morning; rather, we will see it as what we are called to do 24/7 all over the city. In the Ekklesia that Jesus is building, more pastors like Wong Po Ling in Hong Kong will develop "transformation churches" where every *member* is equipped to be a *minister*, and more businesses will use their resources and creativity to share the Gospel with their customers and influence entire industries, as AMENPAPA is doing in the fashion industry.

Share: How can you be a personal example to your local body of believers of how to love the world as much as you (and they) already love the Church? How would your attitudes and actions change toward the people in your city if you started interacting with them as though they were members of your congregation?

_____

_____

Read: The subtitle I chose for chapter 15 suggests that we must move from "commiserating in private to legislating in public." To do so, we must exercise the spiritual authority that Jesus promised us in the Great Commission. But where do we start? In *Ekklesia* I provide several important biblical insights related to the same chapter's main title, "A Fuller Understanding of Spiritual Authority." Let's reconsider them carefully now.

1. It is important that we understand the difference between authority and power. I differentiate them this way in chapter 15:

   There is no question that the devil retains a measure of power in the world today (see 1 John 5:19). The Ekklesia, however, has been granted full *authority* over all the power of the evil one, since it has authority in heaven and on earth (see Matthew 28:18; Luke 10:19). Authority always trumps power. That is why the Scriptures describe Satan as having dominion (power), but never as being a king (authority), because he is not one. A kingdom is a legitimate institution, whereas a domain, or dominion, is something obtained and maintained by force.

2. The authority to cast out demons is bestowed on individuals, but the authority to confront principalities and powers is something that only the Ekklesia can wield. Ephesians 3:10 reveals this principle "so that the manifold wisdom of God might now be made known through the church [the Ekklesia] to the rulers and the authorities in the heavenly places." On this point about the differing levels of authority between individuals and the Church, I present a stern caution both in the book and here: I have seen too many unnecessary casualties in spiritual warfare as a result of well-meaning, very passionate, but biblically misinformed warriors.

3. We must know where our authority comes from and exercise it in the marketplace, first by finding a "point of inception" from which to establish a solid transformation beachhead, and then—and only then—by proceeding forward against the Gates of Hades.

Following the outpouring of the Holy Spirit on the Day of Pentecost, the first significant challenge came the disciples' way when the Sanhedrin tried to silence them from speaking about Jesus. Their response? In Acts 4:19–20, Peter and John replied, "Whether it is right in the sight of God to give heed to you rather than to God, you be the judge; for we cannot stop speaking about what we have seen and heard." They named their authority as God and declared their allegiance to Him in the public square.

4. Spiritual authority that comes from the Father is always accompanied by signs and wonders manifested through the name of Jesus and the power of the Holy Spirit. In the book of Acts, the first believers literally constituted themselves as a legislative assembly (the original function of the secular ekklesia), appealed to the court of heaven and prayed. Notice the power encounter that ensued:

"And now, Lord, take note of their threats, and grant that Your bond-servants may speak Your word with all confidence, while You extend Your hand to heal, and *signs and wonders* take place through the name of Your holy servant Jesus." And when they had prayed, the place where they had gathered together was shaken, and they were all filled with the Holy Spirit and began to speak the word of God with boldness.

And the congregation of those who believed were of one heart and soul; and not one of them claimed that anything belonging to him was his own, but all things were common property to them. And with great power the apostles were giving testimony to the resurrection of the Lord Jesus, and abundant grace was upon them all. For there was not a needy person among them.

Acts 4:29–34, emphasis added

Share: Take a couple of minutes and jot down the amazing outcomes described in these verses, outcomes that were the result of this Ekklesia "legislating" rather than "commiserating." Then share your observations together.

_____

_____

_____

_____

Read: From this powerful point of inception, the authority and impact of Jesus' disciples continued to grow, like the ripple effect that happens when a rock is thrown into a glassy pond. The city streets became "aisles" of ministry, and even Peter's shadow was so full of the Holy Spirit's power that sick people were healed when he passed by. The victory that came through these power encounters resulted in greater authority for the apostles, which in turn led to the ongoing addition of multitudes of new converts: "At the hands of the apostles many signs and wonders were taking place among the people . . . And all the more believers in the Lord, multitudes of men and women, were constantly added to their number" (Acts 5:12–14). This is what properly exercised authority does.

In the years that followed, the apostles experienced supernatural protection, miraculous releases from prison, courage in the face of great danger and abundant grace as all but John became martyrs for their faith. The reality was that the Sanhedrin lost every argument because they were not able to match the Ekklesia's authority.

Every testimony I include in *Ekklesia* bears witness to the fact that spiritual authority serves no purpose until it is exercised. But once it is exercised and a point of inception is established, it becomes a vortex that is progressively filled with growing manifestations of that authority. Look again at some of the points of inception I tell you about throughout the book:

- It began in Ciudad Juárez, Mexico, when Pastor Poncho Murguía put up a tent in a city park and began seeking God for his city.
- It began in the Philippines when Ricardo "King" Flores turned his taxicab into a dwelling place of the Lord.
- It began in Papeete, Tahiti, when architect Francis Oda said yes to God.
- It began in Vallejo, California, when Michael Brown declared that Jesus was the CEO of Michael's Transportation Services.
- It began in Hong Kong when Judge Barbara Chan began prayer-walking her courtroom.
- It began in Honolulu, Hawaii, when Daniel Chinen caught a vision for his high school campus.
- It began in Valley Christian Schools in San Jose, California, when Dr. Cliff Daugherty called on the authority of God to change the spiritual climate on campus.
- It began in Barrio Las Flores, Rosario, Argentina, when Gregorio Avalos ran for president of the neighborhood association and won by four votes.

As I state in chapter 15, "The point of inception is always key—no matter how small it might be—because it shatters darkness. *Darkness* and *hopelessness* are terms that have no plural form, whereas *light* and *hope* do. Once you punch a hole in the darkness, light floods in."

Share: What is a point of inception in your city/region where the light of Jesus, no matter how small, could shatter the darkness?

_____

_____

Deeper: How might you take a next step right now—in your home, your workplace or another possible point of inception—to exercise the spiritual authority God has given you?

_____

_____

Session Summary

- The Ekklesia must love the world as much as God does.
- If our favorite dish is barbecued lamb, God will not send us after the lost sheep.
- An effective witness speaks both grace and truth in all their fullness and in the right biblical sequence.
- "Church" is not just what we do in a building for an hour on Sunday. It is what we do all over the city every day of the week. For that, "church" must become the Ekklesia.
- Signs and wonders in the name of Jesus and by the power of the Holy Spirit always accompany the exercise of genuine spiritual authority.
- Even the smallest amount of light shatters the darkness. "You are the light of the world" (Matthew 5:14).

Transformed Living

Read: Your **Personal Life Application** this week is to claim your spiritual authority and your important role as a marketplace minister, and to ask God to use you to change the spiritual climate in your workplace. This session has reminded us that to love the world the way God loves it, we cannot perceive "church" as something we do inside a building for an hour on Sunday. The Ekklesia that Jesus is building is doing "church" all over the city 24/7. The testimonies I have shared bear this out.

This week as you walk through the door of your workplace, declare either in the Spirit or out loud, "I am a minister! I have the same anointing and authority to do in the marketplace on Monday what my pastor does from the pulpit on Sunday!" Intentionally welcome the Holy Spirit to come. Claim the truth of transformation paradigm #3, "Labor is worship, and since all believers are ministers, they are to turn their jobs into places of worship to God and ministry to others." This prophetic act will fill you with a greater sense of purpose and with confidence that God wants to use you right where you are to bring light, no matter how great the darkness. Make these declarations in your workplace this week and be prepared to report back at your next eGroup meeting.

Your **Group Life Application** this week is to seek God for miracles in the marketplace. In this session we learned that spiritual authority that comes from the Father is always accompanied by signs and wonders manifested through the name of Jesus and the power of the Holy Spirit. These manifestations do not necessarily have to be dramatic or even visible to outsiders, as long as they are life-changing and point the recipient to Jesus if he or she is still unsaved, or to God if the person is already a believer.

Is your eGroup willing to stand in the spiritual authority that God has given you for a miracle that will touch your community with the Good News of the Gospel of the Kingdom? The Lord may lead you to pray for someone who is sick, another person who needs a job, a crisis that needs a divine solution or a marriage that needs saving. How is the Lord speaking to you today? As you move into prayer and ministry time, ask the Holy Spirit to give you faith for something greater than yourselves. He will show you what that is. I encourage you to press in together in order to see what we often consider the "extraordinary" become the "ordinary" in your city. God is faithful, and He will do it. Expect miracles!

Ekklesia Prayer and Ministry

Take time right now to share prayer requests, needs, updates and testimonies before you pray together. As time allows, close with a period of Spirit-led prayer and ministry to one another. Offer prayers of faith, expecting miracles! You can jot down the prayer requests here to help you remember them:

_____

_____

_____

_____

Reading Assignment

In preparation for Session 11, read chapter 16 in *Ekklesia*, "A Fuller Understanding of the Ekklesia's Operational Methodology."

Daily Devotions

Read: Jesus has invited us to take a journey of discovery, faith and empowerment and become more like Him for the sake of the world He loves. We must "go deep" in order to "go wide." The Bible is our playbook. God will call the right plays, but we must know how to run them. Continue to set aside daily time to pray, reflect on the Scriptures provided in these devotions, and apply them to your life. Our commission is carried out "as we go on our way," but following Jesus' example, we recognize that we all need quiet moments to hear from God.

Day One—Romans 1:8–17

Paul highlights his thankfulness for the Christians in Rome and tells them, "Your faith is being proclaimed throughout the whole world" (verse 8). According to verse 11, what does he long to impart to them when he visits? What spiritual gift do you need in order to go deeper with God today? Paul says in verse 16, "For I am not ashamed of the gospel, for it is the power of God for salvation to everyone who believes." Why must we claim this verse in order to move from "commiserating in private to legislating in public"?

Day Two—Luke 15:1–32

Who was Jesus' audience in this Scripture, and what were they objecting to (see verses 1–2)? Jesus mentions three things that were lost. What were they? What is the point of these parables, as related to loving what God loves the most—the world? In the parable of the Prodigal Son, whom do you identify with the most—the older or younger brother? How does the father's response to his son illustrate both grace and truth?

Day Three—Jeremiah 29:4–11

In verses 5–6, what does Jeremiah encourage the Jews in exile to do for their city? Why? Aren't the Babylonians their enemies? In verse 7, God gave the exiles this instruction: "Seek the welfare of the city where I have sent you into exile, and pray to the LORD on its behalf; for in its welfare you will have welfare." In what ways are you seeking the welfare of the city where God has sent you, as He instructed the exiles to do? How does this prophetic direction relate to the first principle of prayer evangelism, which Jesus taught centuries later, in Luke 10?

Day Four—John 14:5–15

On what basis are you qualified to do "greater works" than Jesus (see verse 12)? What is the purpose of Jesus answering your prayer requests for yourself or others (see verse 13)? Do you believe God for miracles? If not, what is holding you back, and how can you bring this obstacle to Jesus and ask Him to remove it?

Day Five—Matthew 5:1–16

How do the Beatitudes found in verses 3–11 represent the "Be-Attitudes" we need in order to walk in the spiritual authority we have received from God? Salt was used in Bible times both to preserve and spice up food (see verse 13). What are you called to "preserve" or "spice up" in the world today? Have you been hiding your light, or are you letting it shine for Jesus, as verses 14–16 direct?

Day Six—1 Corinthians 13:1–13

This passage of the Bible is often called "the Love Chapter." For this reason it is read at many weddings. How does it speak to our witness to the world? What Christlike qualities are we to embrace? Which attitudes and actions do verses 4–6 tell us that we are to reject?

Day Seven—your eGroup meets today! Be blessed!

SESSION 11

What this lesson is about:

There is life in a swamp, but one has to go there to find it. A river is different because it carries life beyond its source. The Ekklesia is called to take life to the world. That is why it must flow like a river. And to break out of the swamp, it must find the banks God has for it. This session focuses on what those banks are and how they lead the Ekklesia to transform the nations.

What you will walk away with:

You will be powerfully energized by the discovery that the transformation of cities *and nations* is no longer a distant hope. Rather, it is a fast-approaching reality, as confirmed by the inspiring prototypes that are emerging from the application of prayer evangelism and the five pivotal paradigms of transformation. Once you grasp and activate these "Jesus principles," as part of His Ekklesia you will be able to bring His presence and His power to bear as an expression of the Kingdom of God—first in your immediate sphere of influence, and eventually in your city and nation, when you learn to flow in a river of transformation that has these biblical banks. What until yesterday looked impossible will become possible because you will have discovered God's methodology to disciple people and nations.

Sharing Life

Watch: Play the video introduction for Session 11. This session is based on chapter 16 in *Ekklesia*, "A Fuller Understanding of the Ekklesia's Operational Methodology."

Pray Together: Dear heavenly Father, Your life-giving Word invites us to "jump in" and flow in the transforming river of the Holy Spirit so that cities and nations can be discipled, starting right where we are. Help us overcome our fears. Show us an entry point. Illuminate the biblical paradigms and principles that lead to sustained transformation. Teach us what Jesus first taught His disciples, so that we might truly be Your Ekklesia today. We welcome Your presence once again because we know that as two or three or more gather in Jesus' name, You are right here with us. In Jesus' name, Amen.

Read: Begin this session by reviewing your **Life Applications** from Session 10.

Share: Your **Personal Life Application** this past week was to claim your spiritual authority and important role as a marketplace minister. We learned that to love the world the way God loves it, we cannot perceive "church" as something we do in a building for an hour on Sunday. The Ekklesia that Jesus is building is doing "church" all over the city 24/7, and the testimonies I have shared bear this out.

I encouraged you to walk through the door of your workplace and declare, either in the Spirit or out loud, "I am a minister! I have the same anointing and authority to do in the marketplace on Monday what my pastor does from the pulpit on Sunday!" And I encouraged you to welcome the Holy Spirit to come into your workplace and begin to change the spiritual climate. Finally, I urged you to claim the truth of transformation paradigm #3, "Labor is worship, and since all believers are ministers, they are to turn their jobs into places of worship to God and ministry to others." Did you claim these promises and make these declarations in your workplace this week? In what way has your attitude toward your workplace changed because of this prophetic act?

_____

_____

_____

What has the spiritual climate been like in your workplace? How would you like to see it change? Have you experienced any immediate changes or "open doors" this week?

_____

_____

_____

_____

Continue to welcome the presence of the Lord into your workplace. Keep claiming your role as a minister in the marketplace. Keep turning your labor into worship as you offer your very best unto the Lord.

Your **Group Life Application** this week was to seek God for miracles in the marketplace. In last week's session, we learned that spiritual authority that comes from the Father is always accompanied by signs and wonders manifested through the name of Jesus and the power of the Holy Spirit. These manifestations do not necessarily have to be dramatic or even visible to outsiders, as long as they are life-changing and point the recipient to Jesus if he or she is still unsaved, or to God if the person is already a believer.

Who or what were you led to offer prayers of faith for as an eGroup? Was it an individual? A group? A particular situation in need of a miracle?

_____

_____

Have your prayers continued throughout the week? What can you report? Are you willing to continue to pray until you get a breakthrough? God is so faithful. Expect miracles!

_____

_____

Transformed Thinking

Read: Transformation is happening millions of times every day all over the world. Thousands of people come to the Lord, lives are changed, churches are planted and wonderful ministry is accomplished in Jesus' name. Why, then, don't we see cities and nations transformed? Could it be that far too often, the Church of today acts more like a swamp than a river? From chapter 16, think of it this way:

> Transformation is like a river. The swamp contains life, but the river *carries* life. The swamp, while nourished by the rain, has no inner movement and is susceptible to stagnation. The river never stagnates. The swamp will take us nowhere. The river's flow will carry us to new horizons with every bend.

What turns a swamp into a river? Banks! Riverbanks provide contour and direction to the river, which, when connected to a constant water source, provide life-giving flow. The two "banks of the river" that have been guiding the flow of the Transform Our World Network, which Ruth and I lead, are prayer evangelism and the five pivotal paradigms for transformation. These two banks have proven themselves to be transcultural, transgenerational and transdenominational. They are not a project, as I say in *Ekklesia*; they are the principles that lay a foundation for every project. They do not constitute a program; they define a lifestyle. They are available and applicable to all, regardless of age, social level, race, color or gender.

Share: When the Church has no outlet for the flow of the Holy Spirit, it can stagnate. What are some factors that can contribute to this?

_____

_____

_____

Read: The first bank of the transformation river, the five pivotal paradigms, define the *what*, *why*, *how*, *where* and *what for* of transformation. They are based on the teachings of Jesus and are indispensable in rediscovering the Ekklesia that Jesus is building as His instrument for global transformation. Let's review them briefly to facilitate some further discussion questions:

Paradigm #1 gives us the *what*: The Great Commission is about discipling nations and not just individuals. "Go therefore and [as you go] make disciples of all the nations" (Matthew 28:19). The God-ordained finish line is discipled nations, and when the finish line is defined properly, everything else begins to make sense. In chapter 16, I write,

> When it finally dawns on us how grand the magnitude and the implications are for what God has called us to do, we will never be able just to settle for a bigger church, a bigger business or a bigger foundation. All of that will become subservient to this much higher calling.

Paradigm #2 gives us the *why*: The Atonement secured redemption not only for individuals, but also for the marketplace, which is the heart of the nation. "For the Son of Man has come to seek and to save that which was lost" (Luke 19:10). Now that Jesus has redeemed the world, His Ekklesia must reclaim it. This is the full scope of the redemptive work of Christ and the authority entrusted to us as God's agents for transformation.

Paradigm #3 gives us the *how*: Labor is worship, and since all believers are ministers, they are to turn their jobs into a place of worship to God and ministry to others. "Whatever you do, do your work heartily, as for the Lord rather than for men" (Colossians 3:23). It is important for us to remember this point that I make in *Ekklesia*: "Nations will be transformed by saints properly trained by their leaders to do the work of the ministry day in and day out as members of Jesus' Ekklesia."

Share: What does it mean to leave the worship switch in the ON position when you go to work?

_____

_____

In what ways is marketplace ministry about more than just our personal fulfillment or success?

_____

_____

Paradigm #4 is about the *where*: Jesus is the One who builds His Church, not us. Our assignment is to use the keys of the Kingdom to lock and unlock the Gates of Hades in order for Him to build His Church where those Gates stand. "I will build My church, and the gates of Hades shall not prevail against it" (Matthew 16:18 NKJV). As I say in this session's chapter,

> Jesus made it crystal clear: "*I* will build *My* church," He said. You and I are not doing the building. And the Gates of Hades will not prevail against it. What are we expected to do? Pick up the keys of the Kingdom, which used to be the keys of Hades and Death, and unlock those gates so that the Ekklesia's building material—saved sinners—will become available.

Paradigm #5 is about the *what for*: The elimination of systemic poverty in its four dimensions—spiritual, relational, motivational and material—is the premier tangible social indicator of transformation. "The Spirit of the Lord is on me, because he has anointed me to proclaim good news to the poor" (Luke 4:18 NIV), and "The Son of God appeared for this purpose, to destroy the works of the devil" (1 John 3:8). The deeper focus of this paradigm is on changing the systems that keep people in poverty. This fifth one opens doors with government officials because they see that we have something valuable to offer that will help them.

Share: Why is it vitally important that we remember that the real Church belongs to Jesus?

_____

_____

Deeper: What "church building material" becomes available when we use the keys of the Kingdom to unlock the Gates of Hades?

_____

_____

Read: The second bank of the transformation river is prayer evangelism. We have found that this four-step methodology, which Jesus taught in the Scriptures, is a most effective way to live out the five pivotal paradigms as a lifestyle. When implemented according to His instructions and by the power of the Holy Spirit, prayer evangelism changes the spiritual climate in your city, starting in you.

In Luke 10, Jesus appointed seventy additional disciples and "sent them in pairs ahead of Him to every city and place where He Himself was going to come" (Luke 10:1). And where were they instructed to go? To the synagogues? No. Rather, to the homes of the people living in those cities. Jesus told them:

> Whatever house you enter, first say, "Peace be to this house." If a man of peace is there, your peace will rest on him; but if not, it will return to you. Stay in that house, eating and drinking what they give you; for the laborer is worthy of his wages. Do not keep moving from house to house. Whatever city you enter and they receive you, eat what is set before you; and heal those in it who are sick, and say to them, "The kingdom of God has come near to you."
>
> Luke 10:5–9

As we have seen before, the four steps of prayer evangelism come out of this passage:

1. *Bless* the lost and speak peace to them (see Luke 10:5).
2. *Fellowship* with them, eating and drinking together (see verse 7).
3. *Minister* to them, taking care of their needs and praying for miracles (see verse 9).
4. *Proclaim*, "The kingdom of God has come near to you" (verse 9).

Share: Since you have already been practicing prayer evangelism during this *Ekklesia* series, what has been your experience so far? How is this teaching helpful? Encouraging? Challenging? Be encouraged that once prayer evangelism becomes a lifestyle for you, what now requires effort and concentration will happen "supernaturally naturally"!

_____

_____

_____

_____

_____

Read: We have covered the basics of prayer evangelism in more than one session, but now let's consider some helpful insights into the importance of each step involved, as a basis for your eGroup discussion. (I delve deeper into each of these insights in chapter 16, which you can refer back to as needed.)

Step #1—Bless, don't blast!

When we bless or "speak peace" in Jesus' name, we pass along an intentional blessing to the intended recipient. The words we speak and the actions we portray, like Jesus' words and actions, should impart "spirit and life." It is important that we speak peace, because too often we have been extremely critical of the lost. As I say in *Ekklesia*, "Preaching the truth without love is like giving someone a kiss when you have bad breath. No matter how good the kiss, no one will come back for a second one."

To bless someone and speak peace to them is to desire God's best for their life. It is to see them as God sees them. The same is true when we choose to bless our neighbor's house, our workplace, our school or City Hall. Blessings cancel the power of the enemy to blind the minds of unbelievers. Romans 16:20 declares, "The God of peace will soon crush Satan under your feet." This is the verse that I told you in the book opened my eyes to a monumental mistake we had been making in spiritual warfare: *We had rated war higher than peace.* It is not the God of war but the God of *peace* who crushes Satan, and He does it under *our* feet—hence the need for us to walk in peace.

Share: Reflect on a person or situation in your life right now where you need to claim the power and perspective of God so that you can "bless," and not "blast." Share this with your eGroup.

_____

_____

Read: Prayer must surround every step of prayer evangelism. Start by "talking to God about your neighbor before talking to your neighbor about God." When you lead with peace and blessing, the Holy Spirit will open the door to Step #2.

Step #2—Engage in two-way fellowship.

Remember, the "social track" that Jesus and subsequently the early Church often used was meals. Think of all the instances of this with Zaccheus, Mary and Martha, the five thousand, the teachers of the Law and Jesus' disciples. When food and fellowship are shared, friendship grows and trust is developed. This step can happen in a variety of ways today, but the desired impact is the same. In chapter 16 I describe it this way:

> Fellowship provides an opportunity to show unconditional acceptance by welcoming people the way they are instead of the way we want them to be.
>
> In fact, Jesus' instruction here is that we let the lost host us. Why? When we allow unbelievers to do something for us, we affirm their value and dignity as God's creation. . . .

Jesus always treated sinners with respect. The worse the sinners, the greater the respect with which He treated them. Think of the cases of Zaccheus and the Samaritan woman; Jesus began His dialogue by asking each of them to do Him a favor. Of Zaccheus he asked a bed and a meal, and of the Samaritan woman He asked water.

Share: Jesus was known as a friend of sinners. How would you rate yourself at being a friend of sinners?

_____

_____

Deeper: When you are fellowshiping with others who don't yet know the Lord, do they pull you down, or do you lift them up?

_____

_____

Step #3—Minister to their felt needs.

As we continue to bless, build relationships and cover the whole encounter with prayer, those we are desiring to reach for Jesus will begin to open up and share their felt needs with us because they sense that we can be trusted or perhaps even have the answer they are looking for. A felt need is a practical, tangible need that is the most pressing in a person's life at the moment: a troubled marriage, a challenging job, a wound from the past or a health concern. We have already been praying *for* these people, but when we minister to their felt needs, the Holy Spirit opens the door for us to pray *with* them. From *Ekklesia*, here is why:

> Prayer is the most tangible trace of eternity in the human heart, and even atheists have prayed in moments of desperation. When you let the lost know that you are praying prayers of faith for their felt needs, you touch them at the heart level.
>
> This is why we must be filled with the Holy Spirit at all times to be able to pray prayers of faith. Divine intervention is the tipping point in prayer evangelism.

Prayers of faith claim the promises of Jesus, who assured us: "He who believes in Me, the works that I do, he will do also; and greater works than these he will do" (John 14:12).

Share: What will happen to someone's heart when he or she sees God answering the prayers you have offered?

_____

_____

Read: Once you have taken the first three steps of blessing someone, fellowshiping and ministering to his or her felt needs, that person will know that God has come near. That opens the door to step #4. Now you can introduce him or her personally to your friend, Jesus.

Step #4—Finally, let the lost know that the Kingdom has come near them, and invite them to come in.

In this step, rather than trying to coerce or convince people into the Kingdom, we are taking the Kingdom to them. In the book I give the example of it being like driving through the desert in an air-conditioned truck stocked with cold drinks. When you spot a weary hiker, you won't need to beg him to come on board; all you need to do is pull over near to him and open the door!

Your assignment is not to convince people that they are sinners or to bring them into the Kingdom of God. Only God can do that. Your assignment is to demonstrate in both words and deeds that God loves them, that Jesus is a present reality, that He cares deeply about them and their circumstances, and that He has just come near to them. When it comes to sharing the Gospel, be ready to "give an account for the hope that is in you" (1 Peter 3:15). Follow the trail that prayer evangelism maps out, and the Holy Spirit will do the rest.

What was the result when the disciples Jesus sent out followed these principles? Luke 10:17–18 reports, "The seventy returned with joy, saying, 'Lord, even the demons are subject to us in your name.' And He said to them, 'I was watching Satan fall from heaven like lightning.'"

There you have it! The result was joy in the journey and victory in Jesus' name. The Gates of Hades were unlocked and the Kingdom of God was released. Why does it work this way? Consider this important observation I make in the book:

> As I searched the Scriptures for a reason why these principles work so unusually well, it dawned on me that both prayer evangelism and the five paradigms come straight out of the teachings of Jesus. Why is this important? Because Jesus was very specific—and to a point even restrictive—when He instructed us to disciple people and nations by "teaching them to observe all that *I commanded you*" (Matthew 28:20, emphasis added).
>
> He did not say, "Teach nations what I will teach Paul, Peter, John and James, who in turn will teach it to you." Instead, Jesus said, "Teach them what *I* have taught and show them how to observe it."

As I also say in the book, the two banks of the river we have been talking about, prayer evangelism and the five pivotal paradigms, work so well because they fluidly connect right doctrine with right application in the right place and sequence.

Share: Evangelism should be a lifestyle, not an assignment that we reluctantly fulfill. Prayer evangelism gives us a different perspective and modus operandi by which we are partnering with the Holy Spirit. Would you like to have more joy in sharing your faith with others? Pause right now and ask the Holy Spirit to plant these transformation paradigms and principles deep in your heart so that the river of God can flow through you. Then make a firm decision to practice these principles until they have become part of your daily routine—in essence, a lifestyle.

Read: The story of transformation in Phuket, Thailand, is another amazing affirmation that these biblical paradigms and principles work in real life. When Pastors Brian and Margaret Burton equipped Wanlapa with an ice-cream scooter and the principles of prayer evangelism, her scooter became a "chariot of fire." Her ice-cream cones became "arrows in the hands of a mighty warrior," and multitudes were evangelized.

You remember the story from reading the chapter. A transformation process was released that affected even the highest-ranking officials in the area. The provincial mayor attended a service in which Pastor Brian was preaching on corruption. The mayor was so personally convicted that he returned a million-dollar bribe, which precipitated others involved in corruption to do likewise. The result was the establishment of a $7 million fund to improve water quality for the citizens of Phuket.

When Pastor Brian, Margaret and their congregation found ways to bless the police chief, relationships developed and doors opened to discovering a huge felt need for more police officers. They prayed, and very soon God blew the police chief out of the water when the federal commissioner in Bangkok called to report that he was authorizing seven thousand new officers for Phuket.

God continued to give divine solutions to ordinary problems, which included a processing center operating "prayer-evangelism style" to help illegal Burmese workers get properly documented. Today, the chain reaction that started with Brian and Margaret Burton and Wanlapa has impacted thousands, with entire villages coming to Christ. It all began when they first taught and then applied these paradigms and principles of transformation with both boldness and complete dependence on the Holy Spirit, expecting miracles.

The result of this kind of lifestyle is that the transformation of cities and nations is no longer a distant hope. Instead, it becomes a fast-approaching reality, as confirmed by the inspiring prototypes we see emerging within the banks of the river. A lifestyle of prayer evangelism is foundational to living out the key pivotal paradigms for transformation that we are called to put into practice as God's Ekklesia and His instrument for global transformation.

Share: What is the "ice-cream scooter" that God has put in your hands as an instrument of transformation?

_____

_____

Session Summary

- Transformation is like a river that carries life beyond its source.
- The two banks of this river, consisting of biblical paradigms and principles that Jesus taught, provide contour and direction that lead to sustainable and expandable transformation.
- The application of the five pivotal paradigms is key to rediscovering God's instrument for global transformation—His Ekklesia.
- Prayer evangelism is meant to be the lifestyle through which we implement the five pivotal paradigms for transformation in our daily lives.
- The tipping point of prayer evangelism is divine, miraculous intervention in the lives of those we are trying to reach for Jesus, and it begins through our blessing them and fellowshiping with them "a la Luke 10."
- When we follow Jesus' teachings, we will experience joy similar to His joy when He saw "Satan fall down." By this we mean that the change prayer evangelism produces in the spiritual climate will dislodge the principalities and powers that are polluting the atmosphere and blinding sinners to the light of the Gospel.

Transformed Living

Read: Your **Personal Life Application** is unique this time. If you live within walking or driving distance of a river in your region, I encourage you to go there for a time of prayer, reflection and a review of the operational methodology of the Ekklesia, along with a soul-searching assessment of your current relationship with God. You may want to go with a friend, but each of you can find your own quiet space.

Start with prayer. Now picture one of the riverbanks you are looking at as the five pivotal paradigms and the other as the principles of prayer evangelism. Notice how they provide contour and direction to the river. Observe the flow of the water. Imagine it as "life-giving water" that represents the forward movement of God's Spirit transforming the world. Now imagine yourself floating in that river, carried by the Spirit and safe in the arms of Jesus, fulfilling your unique purpose as a member of Jesus' Ekklesia.

As you share in this very visual and personal time of reflection, let the Holy Spirit speak to you. What have you learned during this *Ekklesia* study?

What has God impressed deep within your heart? What change may yet be required? Have you said yes to God for the next steps? Jot down any insights you receive so that you can share them with your eGroup.

_____

_____

_____

_____

_____

_____

Now go deeper by asking some soul-searching questions about your relationship with God. We cannot *proclaim* the Gospel of the Kingdom to others, step #4 of prayer evangelism, if we have not received and benefitted from this Good News in our own lives. We cannot share "righteousness and peace and joy in the Holy Spirit" if we don't have the Holy Spirit filling us with these gifts. No one can borrow a shirt from someone who has no clothes. We must have something desirable to offer to the lost. Reflect on the following questions and others as the Spirit prompts. You may wish to journal some of your thoughts on the lines provided.

Do you ever find that you are more focused on doing the religious thing than on growing in your intimacy with Jesus?

Do you have a burden for the lost, and do you have a vision for the transformation of your city?

Have you experienced miracles or divine interventions in your ministry?

Are there areas of secret sin in your life that are creating a stronghold?

Do you endeavor to "right what is wrong" when you encounter injustice? If not, why not?

Is your work and your worship more of a "have to" than a "want to"?

Do you experience the peace of God in your heart even during very stressful times?

What gives you the greatest joy in life? Does this joy flow from your relationship with Jesus?

What do you need God to do for you right now? Ask Him! What do you need to do for God? Tell Him!

_____

_____

_____

_____

_____

_____

_____

Your **Group Life Application** this week is to plan an eGroup celebration either at the conclusion of Session 12 next week or at a special time in the near future. The purpose of this celebration will be to thank God for this *Ekklesia* study, for the relationships that you have built through it and for the good deeds through which you have already had an impact on your personal spheres of influence, your city and your region.

Another purpose of your celebration will be to consider your next steps as a group. I encourage you to multiply and grow forward using the additional resources available at www.transformourworld.org. They will take you deeper and wider as you seek to become Jesus' Ekklesia and disciple cities and nations.

Discuss your ideas for this celebration now and plan a fun fellowship opportunity, a meal, a special time of worship and prayer, or all of the above as a fitting conclusion to this twelve-week journey that you have shared together of *Ekklesia: Rediscovering God's Instrument for Global Transformation*. Jot down the details of your celebration here:

_____

_____

_____

Ekklesia Prayer and Ministry

Take time right now to share prayer requests, needs, updates or testimonies before you pray together. As time allows, close with a period of Spirit-led prayer and ministry to one another. You can jot down the prayer requests here to help you remember them:

_____

_____

_____

_____

_____

Reading Assignment

In preparation for Session 12, read chapter 17 in *Ekklesia*, "The Way Forward."

Daily Devotions

Read: The Scriptures and devotional thoughts that follow will once again prompt further reflection and application of the key themes we shared in this session. A daily commitment to time in God's Word should continue long after this Ekklesia study concludes. The apostle Paul encourages us, "Put on the full armor of God, so that you will be able to stand firm against the schemes of the devil" (Ephesians 6:11). Then he adds that to resist the evil one, we should take up "the sword of the Spirit, which is the word of God" (verse 17). Take up your sword right now and win the battle!

Day One—Psalm 46:1–11

This beautiful psalm begins, "God is our refuge and strength, a very present help in trouble. Therefore we will not fear . . ." (verses 1–2). Think of an area of your life where God is these things for you. The psalmist continues, "There is a river whose streams make glad the city of God" (verse 4). Picture how pleased God will be when all the streams of Christianity flow together in the river that leads to the transformation of nations! Verse 10 says, "Cease striving and know that I am God." Where do you need to let go and just trust God?

Day Two—Romans 12:1–8

What do you think Paul means when he says in verse 1, "Present your bodies a living and holy sacrifice . . . your spiritual service of worship"? What might this have to do with claiming your calling as a minister in the marketplace? According to verse 2, once God has our hearts, what else would He like to transform? Why? Verse 6 says, "Since we have gifts that differ according to the grace given to us, each of us is to exercise them accordingly . . ." As examples, Paul lists prophecy, service, teaching, exhorting, giving, leading, showing mercy and being cheerful. What gifts are you using to serve God?

Day Three—Isaiah 60:1–3

I encourage you to claim the prophetic words of this passage, fulfilled according to God's perfect plan, through the life of Jesus. He declared, "I am the Light of the world" (John 8:12). What does Isaiah 60:1 promise to those who choose to walk in this light? What about for those walking in darkness (see verse 2)? For nations (see verse 3)? According to Revelation 21:24, this is the vision that will be fulfilled at the throne of God one day: "The nations will walk by its light, and the kings of the earth will bring their glory into it."

Day Four—Ecclesiastes 3:1–15

Consider verses 1–8 of this passage. What "appointed time" or season is it in your life? Where are you in your journey as a follower of Jesus Christ? What does it mean as we reach out to unbelievers that God has "set eternity in their heart" (verse 11)? If you are in agreement with verse 14, that "everything God does will remain forever," how will this affect your decisions and priorities about your use of time?

Day Five—1 Thessalonians 4:13–18

Have you ever been to a funeral with a group of people who are totally "uninformed" about Jesus and who therefore are grieving with "no hope," as verse 13 talks about? What is the message of hope contained in this passage? How would you share it with someone who does not yet know Christ? Verse 18 concludes, "Therefore comfort one another with these words." How does the encouragement in this passage link with the four steps of prayer evangelism?

Day Six—Philippians 4:4–9

Why do you think that Paul repeats his admonition in verse 4 to rejoice? Stress is a killer. What is Paul's recipe in verse 6 for being "anxious about nothing"? According to verse 7, what is God's promise when we follow this plan of action? What things does verse 8 say we are to dwell on? Why? Consider verse 9. Who are your examples in life?

Day Seven—your eGroup meets today! Be blessed!

SESSION 12

How do we transition from the Church to the Ekklesia? It is a challenge because what we have in the Church today is good, but in order to become the Ekklesia, we have to make room for the "much more" of God. In this session and chapter 17 of the book, I present the pathway to that transition.

You will see that God has a hope and a future for you, but it is not just about you, it is about the world—the peoples and the nations for which Jesus died. What He has prepared for you is beyond anything you can think or imagine. You may find yourself perplexed, just as Mary did when she asked, "How can this be, since I am a virgin?" (Luke 1:34). The answer she got is the same one God wants to give you: "The Holy Spirit will come upon you, and the power of the Most High will overshadow you" (Luke 1:35).

At the very end of *Ekklesia*, I invite you to dream with me about your nation. Did you picture its flag waving in the wind of the Spirit and carried by its president or prime minister, bowing before God Almighty? Watching this scenario, can you recognize your part in bringing it all about through your obedience to His call?

In your study of *Ekklesia*, have you committed to journey toward the final destination of seeing multitudes saved and nations discipled? I also say at the end of the book that in every journey—no matter how long—the most important step is the first one because it represents commitment to its final destination. As you envision where you are headed on this journey, are you letting the Holy Spirit baptize you afresh and anew with power *and with fire*? Are you letting the two most powerful words in His Kingdom spring from your lips? "Yes, Lord!" As you and I and others commit ourselves to doing that, Jesus' Ekklesia will arise!

Sharing Life

Watch: Play the video introduction for Session 12. This session is based on chapter 17 in *Ekklesia*, "The Way Forward."

Pray Together: Dear God, You have brought us so far as we have studied *Ekklesia*. We are inspired by its teaching. Help us continue to apply the biblical principles illuminated within this series to our daily lives. We thank You and praise You for the love we have shared in our eGroup and for the deep relationships we have built. May they continue into the future, for the purpose of having even greater impact for the Kingdom of God and the discipling of nations. Show us the way forward. Fill us with the love of Jesus. Empower us by your Holy Spirit. Raise our expectations for the miraculous. Use us, we pray, to be Your Ekklesia here on earth! In Jesus' name, Amen.

Read: Begin this session by reviewing your **Life Applications** from Session 11.

Your **Personal Life Application** for this past week was to go to a river in your area and review, reflect and pray about the operational methodology of the Ekklesia that you studied in chapter 16, along with doing a soul-searching assessment of your current relationship with God. We acknowledged that we cannot proclaim the Gospel of the Kingdom and share "righteousness and peace and joy in the Holy Spirit" if we don't first have these gifts present in our own hearts. Were you able to find the time to complete this very visual exercise of prayer and reflection? If so, share some of the answers to the following questions with your eGroup.

Where did you go? What did you observe in the river that relates to the two banks of the river we talked about—prayer evangelism and the five pivotal paradigms for transformation?

_____

_____

How did the Holy Spirit speak to you about the insights you gained and the next steps in your transformation journey?

_____

_____

When you told the Lord what you needed the most, did He answer your prayer?

_____

_____

How will this exercise help prepare you to proclaim the Gospel of the Kingdom more effectively?

_____

_____

Your **Group Life Application** this week was to plan an eGroup celebration as both a conclusion to this twelve-week *Ekklesia* series and as a springboard to the future. Is your celebration today, or have you made plans for a future gathering? I will say more at the end of this session to encourage you to multiply and grow forward.

Transformed Thinking

Read: This concluding session presents several practical steps of application, along with important transition points that will take us from the Church as usual to the "much more" that God has in store for the Ekklesia. We will also consider the importance of taking a first step, which many of you have already done, with the "measure of faith" God has given you. As we saw in chapter 17, a measure of faith, when acted on in obedience, leads to an even greater measure of faith, which in turn leads to an opportunity for greater works. This cycle, coupled with the transforming power of the Holy Spirit, is how God has set things up for us to fulfill the Great Commission and disciple nations. What a privilege to be on God's team!

In the final chapter of *Ekklesia*, I offer several insights that can help you turn the principles you have learned into action, whether you are a pastor or a marketplace minister. One of the most important of these is the "5-15-80 percent principle." It is vital to incorporate this principle as you look for allies and partners in this new transformation venture. Remember that people generally fall into one of three categories:

- *The 5 percent who are visionaries.* These are the "immediate adopters" who see the vision immediately and embrace it by faith.

- *The 15 percent who are implementers.* These are the "early adopters" who are ready to join the visionaries to make it happen.

- *The 80 percent who are maintainers.* These are the "late adopters" who need to see the vision becoming reality in order to get on board.

Start by implementing prayer evangelism and the five pivotal paradigms for transformation in your life, and then identify the 5 percent who are *visionaries* and who will join you immediately. Next, solicit their help in discovering the 15 percent who are *implementers* and who will help you implement a transformation vision in your congregation, workplace or community. Finally, be assured that the 80 percent who are *maintainers* will gladly join you when they can see tangible results. Here is a word from the book about that process:

> As you begin to implement transformation principles, follow the 5-15-80 percent principle. Don't stop what you are already doing with and for the 80 percent, the maintainers, or you may lose them. Just do the "new" with the 5-15 percent group, because they will not mind adding to their current workload. And once the other 80 percent see transformation taking place, they will swing your way.

In our movement, we lead with prototypes and not just principles or ideas. Many people preach about principles without showing how the principles actually work. The strength of our movement is that we do both, teaching the principles *and* implementing them so that people can see and believe them. We search the Scriptures, listen to the Holy Spirit for what He is saying to the Ekklesia, articulate it, validate it biblically, and then we implement it for the benefit of all.

Here are some other helpful and important insights I mention in the concluding chapter of *Ekklesia*:

- *Seek cohesiveness before inclusiveness.* Establish a strong core group in your local church, marketplace setting or community that shares this "transformation DNA" before going too wide with the vision. This will give you a strong foundation to build upon.
- *Make purpose the "driver" instead of unity.* Unity is important, but it can become an end in itself. The key is to find "unity with a purpose," whose higher goal is always transforming a city and nation (see Psalm 133 and John 17:20–21).
- *Seek committed people who can grow in competence.* This is where ongoing training is so important, utilizing the transformation resources that are available.
- *Recognize that God has favorites and you are one of them.* We are all equal at the foot of the cross, but God does pick and choose when it comes to ministry assignments.

Yes, you are a favorite with God. Take note of this point that I make about that in chapter 17:

> The devil will point out that you are not the best candidate, and for once he may be right! There are likely many—perhaps thousands out there—who are better qualified for the task at hand, and who have more resources and better training. But the criterion is not whether we are the best, but whether we are the anointed ones, the chosen ones, as the direct result of God's sovereign choice to bestow unmerited grace on us.

Share: Can you relate to this statement? Are there times when you have felt inadequate for the tasks God is calling you to? On the other hand, where have you been sensing God's anointing on your life?

Which of these three categories—visionaries, implementers or maintainers—would you put yourself in, and why?

Deeper: If you recognize that you are an implementer or a maintainer, both of which are just as much gifts from the Lord as visionaries, ask yourself, *Is there a visionary with whom I could share the* Ekklesia *book and study guide to help light a fire for transformation?* Make a note here to remind yourself to do that with whoever comes to mind.

Read: It may have surprised you to learn that the membership of Jesus' Ekklesia is not limited to the number of people on your local church membership rolls or the combined total of believers in your community, or even in the entire world. Jesus' Ekklesia consists of all believers here on earth and all believers who have already gone on to heaven. Hebrews 12:1 declares, "Therefore, since we have so great a cloud of witnesses surrounding us, let us also lay aside every encumbrance and the sin which so easily entangles us, and let us run with endurance the race that is set before us."

Witnesses, by their very nature, must be able to see or hear something and testify about it. You can have confidence that this heavenly "cheerleading team" is a growing, proactive group of supporters cheering on the forward movement of the Ekklesia here on earth, to the point that you can also say, as I do in the book, "My fellow Kingdom soldier, we are part of a larger, stronger and mightier army. Let us engage the enemy. Victory is assured."

Share: Why is it important to catch this expansive vision of Jesus' Ekklesia?

Read: How do we move from the ordinary to the extraordinary? It is a question I raise both at the start and the finish of *Ekklesia*, and I want to say one more time that the issue is not so much what we are doing wrong, but what else needs to be done. Once more, here is the list of transition points drawn from the teachings in this book and reiterated in these twelve sessions. Each point is followed by an observation I make about it in the book. These are the points that can move us from doing what is good to stepping up to a more excellent way. To move from the ordinary to the extraordinary, transition . . .

- *From personal salvation to household salvation.* The engine for this transition is the realization that "it is not about you" but about others, specifically about everybody in your sphere of influence, including your family, neighbors, workers and others. God's grace has been entrusted to you so that you can pass it on to others.

- *From doing church once a week to being the Ekklesia 24/7.* All the wonderful, life-changing things that happen inside the church building should be happening all over the city—and even more things.

- *From pastoring believers to shepherding the city.* It is the shepherd who looks after the lost sheep, not the other way around. Prayer evangelism is the operational "rod" in the hand of that shepherd: to bless, fellowship, minister and then proclaim. As my close associate Dave Thompson likes to say, "Speak peace and follow the trail!" It has never been easier to pastor a city.

- *From preaching with words to proclaiming with deeds.* The Gospel of the Kingdom is not proclaimed so much with words, but with deeds, to bring about justice, peace and joy. The Savior who brought those to your life is also the Savior of the entire world.

- *From saving souls to discipling nations.* The spiritual empowerment it requires to believe God for nations comes from a clearer vision of the cross and the resulting understanding of everything that took place there. Jesus paid the price for everything that was lost, but He also categorically defeated the devil and made a public spectacle of him and his principalities and powers. The Savior rendered him powerless. God knows it. Jesus knows it. The devil knows it. And now that you know it, act on it! *Bapto* your nation by claiming it for God, and then establish God's authority in a point of inception from where, like leaven injected into dough, it will progressively expand.

- *From contemplating God to partnering with God.* It is biblically proven that we play a vital role in God's plans, and to do that, we must move from contemplation of the divine to partnership with

God. In the same way, Jesus declared even as a young lad, "I must be about My Father's business" (Luke 2:49 NKJV). Like Him, we must be about our Father's business.

- *From water baptism to Holy Spirit baptism.* Without the baptism of the Holy Spirit, we can do nothing either at the personal or the Ekklesia level. That is why we say that the *baptism in the Holy Spirit is the indispensable source of power for the Ekklesia*, and through the Ekklesia, to disciple individuals and cities and nations.

- *From going to church to becoming Jesus' Ekklesia.* The entire creation is eagerly awaiting the manifestation of God's children, and the Ekklesia is that platform. The New Testament presents God as our Father. We are His children, and the world is waiting for us to "come out of the closet."

Share: What part of your city has God uniquely called you to shepherd? What next steps should you take as an eGroup to see God's Kingdom manifested in your city and beyond?

_____

_____

_____

_____

_____

Why is the baptism of the Holy Spirit "*the indispensable source of power for the Ekklesia*"? Are you operating with that power source in your life? Continue to ask God for fresh outpourings of the Holy Spirit so that you personally go from dipping to dripping, as we talked about in Session 8.

_____

_____

Deeper: It is important to reflect on, embrace and contextualize all these transition points as you move forward, because they are essential in rediscovering Jesus' Ekklesia. Right now, however, share which of these transition points has really been speaking to you personally.

_____

_____

Read: I point out in *Ekklesia* that, generally speaking, many of today's churches more often resemble the synagogue than the Ekklesia. They are effective centers of worship, fellowship, Bible study and service, but they are not as effective in relating to the culture in the marketplace and reaching the millions who don't yet know Jesus, let alone becoming effective at discipling cities and nations.

In Session 9, we saw that the tipping point came for the apostle Paul when he left the synagogue, set up shop in the marketplace, showed people how to lead their whole household to faith and established the Ekklesia where people lived and worked. The powerful implication is that if we are willing to rediscover the Ekklesia today and take the Church to the world, we could experience another Acts 18 phenomenon where a God-fearing Gentile like Crispus could come to the Lord and trigger an explosion of myriads of people coming to Christ. Would we be ready to see them baptized immediately in water and the Holy Spirit? Would we welcome them into the New Testament Ekklesia, which will be identified more with the marketplace than with the local congregation? These are questions we must ponder since they involve each of us.

You have read these words more than once in my book and in this study: "Without God we can't, but without us He won't." It is an intriguing point in our partnership with Him. It entails both a privilege and a responsibility for which we are to give an account: "For we must all appear before the judgment seat of Christ, so that each one may be recompensed for his deeds in the body, according to what he has done, whether good or bad" (2 Corinthians 5:10).

Ephesians 2:10 reveals God's blueprint for our lives: "For we [you] are His workmanship, created in Christ Jesus for good works, which God prepared beforehand so that we [you] would walk in them" (Ephesians 2:10). In one more comment from the book, let me tell you again,

> This is a three-part *God*, one-part *you* recipe. He created you, He saved you and He has a plan for your life. His three parts are already in place. Now you have to begin to walk in His plan. That plan consists of good works He has prepared beforehand, which, like a series of motion-activated lights along a path, do not come on until you take the first step. At that moment the first light comes on, and as you progress, the following ones light up in succession. All you have to do is begin to walk and keep on walking.

Take that all-important first step of committing to the journey and to its final destination. Step into it by becoming a voice for the future rather than an echo of the past. Rediscover Jesus' Ekklesia, the real Church He is building, and discover your vital and exciting part in it!

Share: As we conclude this study, pause in your eGroup right now and take some quiet moments to let the Holy Spirit speak to you. Then tell Him the most powerful words in His Kingdom: "Yes, Lord!"

Session Summary

- Whatever "measure of faith" God has already given you for discipling nations, know that as you step out in faith, obedience and good works, He will exchange the faith you have now for a "greater measure of faith" for the journey ahead.

- The first step is to say yes to God. The second step is to start right where you are to practice prayer evangelism and implement the teaching of Jesus regarding His Ekklesia.

- Recognize that you are God's anointed one, whom He has chosen to do great things for His Kingdom. Be humble, but don't be afraid to roar like a lion when the occasion calls for it!

- Pay attention to the transition points needed for the Church today to move it from the "as is" to the "much more" that God has in store—from the ordinary to the extraordinary. Continue to ask yourself, *What paradigms need to shift in my mind and in my heart?*

- Go public for Jesus! Take your faith from the church building into the marketplace of everyday life.

- In all things, depend fully on the Word of God, the power of the cross and the fullness of the Holy Spirit. Go for it in Jesus' name!

Transformed Living

Read: Your **Personal Life Application** this week is to prayerfully consider God's "way forward" for you as a vital member of Jesus' Ekklesia, God's instrument for global transformation. Here are some specific recommendations:

- Continue to practice the principles of prayer evangelism as a lifestyle.

- Continue to reflect on, embrace and contextualize the transition points summarized throughout *Ekklesia* in order to move from the "as is" to the "much more," from the ordinary to the extraordinary.

- If you have not yet done so, please join the movement by clicking on "JOIN" at www.transformourworld.org. Also *Adopt Your Street* and sign up for "Transformation on Demand" so that you can continue being inspired by the life-changing testimonies of the Ekklesia at work around the world.

- Above all, seek the presence and power of the Holy Spirit for each continuing step of this journey of transformation. Remember that "the path of the righteous is like the light of dawn, that shines brighter and brighter until the full day" (Proverbs 4:18).

Your **Group Life Application** this week is to continue your discussion about next steps, as well as enjoying your eGroup celebration to thank

God and fellowship together. Your group leader will inform you about the availability of a growing array of resources and mentoring opportunities, many of them free, to help you continue to flow between the two banks of the river. I encourage you to continue building on the **Life Applications** and resulting projects that were part of this series.

The goal for every eGroup is that it would grow and multiply itself by forming new groups, recognizing that the Ekklesia is an organism designed to operate 24/7 in the marketplace. If your group met within your local church, consider new opportunities to establish Ekklesias in a business, school, home or other location in your city. Is there a member of your group right now who is feeling called to start a new group? Talk about it together. Your group leader will assist you, as may others who are providing direction or oversight.

The ongoing transformation journey is a team effort as we partner with others to grow the Kingdom of God. What does God love the most? The world! Jesus launched the Ekklesia, serving as its Head, so that we could be His hands and feet and reclaim everything that He has already redeemed!

Ekklesia Prayer and Ministry

Take time right now to share prayers of praise and thanksgiving for all that God has done through your twelve sessions together, both within your hearts and in your communities. Say "Yes, Lord!" and then lift up your next steps so that "He who began a good work in you will perfect it until the day of Christ Jesus" (Philippians 1:6). Share in Spirit-led prayer and ministry, as time allows.

Daily Devotions

Read: I encourage you to continue a daily discipline of Bible reading, reflection and application, all of it bathed in prayer. During this series we have considered dozens of compelling and relevant Scripture passages, yet we have just scratched the surface. Continue to dig deep and be blessed!

Day One—Hebrews 12:1–3

In light of the fact that our "cheering section" is much larger than we may have realized, how do verses 1–2 encourage us to run the race? What does it mean to you to "fix your eyes on Jesus" in every circumstance? What is an "encumbrance" of sin that is entangling your life right now that you are ready to lay aside? Ask God to help you do it right now. What will keep you from growing weary and losing heart (see verse 3)?

Day Two—2 Corinthians 4:7–18

Have you been afflicted, crushed, perplexed, persecuted and struck down in your life? You are in good company! So had been the apostle Paul. Yet he preached the Gospel, and he declared, "Therefore we do not lose heart" (verse 16). God has a plan! You are a part of it! Keep your eyes on things that are eternal, as verse 18 says. You belong to Jesus' Ekklesia, and He already won the victory.

Day Three—Matthew 16:13–28

As we finish this twelve-part series on Jesus' Ekklesia, would you answer Jesus' question in verse 15 any differently today? "But who do you say that I am?" Claim again Jesus' amazing promises about His Ekklesia in verses 18–19. In verses 22–23, how did Peter so quickly become a "stumbling block" to a plan of salvation greater than he was able to comprehend? What is the cost of discipleship that Jesus describes in verses 24–26? Are you ready to pay this cost?

Day Four—Hebrews 13:1–8

As we continue today in Hebrews, the writer declares in verse 8, "Jesus Christ is the same yesterday and today and forever." In a world that is constantly changing, does this verse bring you confidence and comfort? Make a list of everything you are encouraged to "continue" doing in verses 1–7 to walk in this confidence and comfort every day.

Day Five—Isaiah 40:28–31

What things make you tired and weary? Family responsibilities? Work demands? Community involvements? How good it is to know that your God never becomes weary or tired (verse 28). As a matter of fact, when you "wait for the Lord" and don't merely rely on your own human strength, He will give you renewed strength to "mount up with wings like eagles" so that you can soar. You will "run and not get tired," and you will "walk and not become weary" (verse 31). This is the God we serve!

Day Six—Psalm 121:1–8

As you take the next steps forward in your personal transformation journey and continue to partner with others as a member of Jesus' Ekklesia, know where your help comes from: "from the Lord, who made heaven and earth" (verses 1–2). Our God is on duty 24/7/365 and "will protect you from all evil; He will keep your soul" (verse 7).

Remember that you have at your disposal a toolbox full of the four indispensable tools I mentioned several times in the videos you watched. Don't forget to use these tools!

1. *The Word of God.* The Word is irreplaceable, providing a solid foundation for you. When you read it, ask yourself these three questions: *What does it say?* (Observation.) *What does it mean?* (Interpretation.) *What does it mean to me?* (Application.)

2. *The Holy Spirit in you.* The Holy Spirit is your Comforter, your Teacher and your Guide on this transformation journey.

3. *The power to pull down strongholds.* As we have talked about many times throughout this study, the Gates of Hades will *not* prevail against Jesus' Ekklesia!

4. *The faith for extraordinary miracles.* Be full of expectation as you take the Good News into your sphere of influence, because miracles are God's normal behavior!

"As you go" forward to fulfill the Great Commission—the Great Partnership—claim this promise: "The LORD will guard your going out and your coming in from this time forth and forever" (verse 8).

Day Seven—You are the Ekklesia! You are God's instrument for global transformation—the real Church Jesus is building!

Dr. Ed Silvoso is the founder and president of Harvest Evangelism Inc. and also of the Transform Our World Network, which is composed of thousands of pulpit and marketplace influencers across the globe. He is widely recognized as a visionary strategist and solid Bible teacher who specializes in nation and marketplace transformation.

Dr. Silvoso has been trained both in theology and business, and his work experience includes banking, hospital administration, financial services and church ministry. As a strategic thinker with a passion to equip ordinary people to do extraordinary things, he has spent his lifetime mining life-giving biblical principles for transformation and linking them to practical application for Christians so that they will see transformation impact their lives, families, spheres of influence and, ultimately, their cities and nations.

Dr. Silvoso's bestselling books on the topic of transformation have become groundbreaking classics. His DVD series *Transformation in the Marketplace with Ed Silvoso* provides tangible validation of the transformation principles at work by documenting prototypes now being developed on every continent.

Dr. Silvoso and his wife, Ruth, have four married daughters and twelve grandchildren. For more details on his life and ministry, see the Wikipedia article "Ed Silvoso" at http://en.wikipedia.org/wiki/Ed_Silvoso. You can also find Dr. Silvoso online at www.transformourworld.org or www.edsilvoso.com. Contact him at Edsilvoso@transformourworld.org, or visit him at

Facebook

www.facebook.com/transformourworld
www.facebook.com/EdSilvoso

Twitter

@transfrmourwrld
@edsilvoso

Instagram

EdSilvoso

More from Ed Silvoso

Visit edsilvoso.com to learn more about Ed, his ministry and his books.

The role of women in the Church is hotly debated, even today. Here Ed Silvoso offers his response to this issue, persuasively presenting the Bible's portrayal of women as powerful adversaries of the devil. There is no doubt that women have a pivotal place in God's plan for Satan's ruin. And there is no doubt that we, the united Body of Christ, will triumph in His name.

Women: God's Secret Weapon

God loves us and has a unique blueprint for our lives, but it's up to us to live it out. Mingling stories and biblical anecdotes with practical advice, Silvoso shows how God intervenes to transform people and nations today. As he helps you discover your own specific purpose, you'll learn that God has great things planned for you!

Transformation

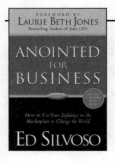

In this bestselling book, Ed Silvoso invites the Church to engage with the heart of our cities: the marketplace. With biblical examples and extraordinary true stories, he shows us how to knock down the perceived wall between commercial pursuit and service to God—and participate in an unparalleled marketplace transformation.

Anointed for Business

✓Chosen

 Stay up to date on your favorite books and authors with our free e-newsletters. Sign up today at chosenbooks.com.

 Find us on Facebook. facebook.com/chosenbooks

 Follow us on Twitter. @Chosen_Books